GARLIC

GARLIC

101 savory and seductive recipes, along with fascinating facts and folklore

by Sue Kreitzman

A Particular Palate Cookbook
Harmony Books/New York

**For Lloyd John Harris,
whose scholarship and garlic passion
have been an inspiration**

A Particular Palate Cookbook

Copyright © 1984 by Sue Kreitzman.

Published by Harmony Books, a division of Crown Publishers, Inc., One Park Avenue, New York, New York 10016, and simultaneously in Canada by General Publishing Company Limited

HARMONY, PARTICULAR PALATE, and colophons are trademarks of Crown Publishers, Inc.

Manufactured in the United States of America

Page 59, recipe from *Food and Wine* magazine, copyright © May 1983, used by permission.

Page 56, recipe from *From the Market-to-Kitchen Cookbook,* by Perla Meyers, used with permission.

Library of Congress Cataloging on Publication Data

Kreitzman, Sue.
  Garlic.

  1. Cookery (Garlic)   I. Title.
TX819.G3K74 1984   641.6′526   83-26451
ISBN 0-517-53314-7 (pbk.)

10 9 8 7 6 5 4 3 2 1

First Edition

Contents

Acknowledgments

Many people contributed support, recipes, advice, and nuggets of history and folklore to this book. I particularly want to thank the following.

Carol Saunders from the Fresh Garlic Association: Carol provided me with several dandy ideas for cooking whole garlic as well as the Pasta Primavera recipe. In addition, she provided Garlic Soufflé, Eggplant Orientale, Sole Verte au Provence; and Garlic Broccoli Salad, American Café—all from her excellent booklet, *Great Garlic Recipes from Great American Chefs*.

Lloyd John Harris: his *Book of Garlic*, his *Garlic Times*, and his dedication to and knowledge of garliciana has been a constant inspiration.

Perla Meyers: her culinary inventiveness and her love of garlic are legendary. Her generosity with garlic advice and with two recipes, Roast Chicken in Sherry Vinegar and Garlic, and Braised Leg of Lamb Arlesienne, is much appreciated.

Julie Coppedge: she and the Televideo computer, in close partnership, produced a beautiful manuscript, right on time.

I also wish to thank: Patrick Burke and César Maggio of Patrick's Café, Robert Charles of La Vieille Maison, Jimella Lucas of The Ark, Maryanne Threadgill and the Placitas Garlic Consortium, Joseph deAssereto of Cantina D'Italia, Warren Picower and Anne Disrude of the *Food and Wine* magazine Andrea Smith, Happy Baker of The Happy Baker Cooking School, Madelene Hill of Hilltop Herb Farm, Walter Coppedge, Paul and Ann Masselli, Frank and Amy Ma, Christiane Lauterbach, Ron Cohn, and Connie Richardson.

Finally, much love and many thanks to the Knife & Fork team for their patience, and to my family: my husband, Steve, for his love and support, his savvy with the Wordstar word processor and his constant and uplifting enthusiasm for my work; my son, Shawm, for his music, his good humor, and outrageous puns; and my beagle Shallot, who thinks that I cook like an angel and is always ready to taste something new.

Garlic in History

From the beginning of recorded time, a cluster of small cloves with powerful taste and pervasive perfume has flavored humanity's history, literature, and religion even more thoroughly than its stews and sauces. Over the centuries, *Allium sativum*—garlic— has been embraced as a sort of super nostrum and mystical charm. It has been reputed to cure a myriad of diseases and ailments from plague and hypertension to toothaches and severe colds; used as a deterrent to snakes, scorpions, vampires, and the evil eye; depended upon to build health, strength, virility, and to increase longevity. On the other hand, garlic has been reviled as vulgar peasant food, deadly poison, an inciter of lust, and the cause of intolerable halitosis.

Pliny, the Roman naturalist, recommended it for sixty-one different maladies, including hemorroids, shrewmouse bite, epilepsy, and hoarseness. Hippocrates liked the bulb for treatment of leprosy and chest pains; Aristotle found it a dandy cure for hydrophobia; and the ancient Persians thought it would stimulate the growth of hair in bald men. But during this time of pharmaceutical activity, garlic as a culinary ingredient was often either ignored or despised.

Fortunately, things have changed. Food lovers have clasped the versatile bulb to their bosoms with fervent enthusiasm; in fact, we are in the midst of a garlic revolution. Chefs all around the country, many of them proponents of the much touted "New American Cuisine," are creating innovative dishes using great quantities of garlic. There is good reason for this sudden upsurge; America's cooking community has finally realized that garlic can be a gentle vegetable, a succulent bulb, a cache of subtly flavored, tender nuggets. Its flavor can be at once soothing and seductive and it can blend with other ingredients, both sweet and savory, in a way that is neither overpowering nor self-effacing.

Garlic hasn't changed, but our understanding of it has. We have learned what many other national groups have known for a long time: garlic has a gentle and tender potential.

The revolution began, as so many American culinary revelations did, with James Beard. He demonstrated the gentle goodness of chicken braised with forty cloves of garlic, and his students took it to heart, talking about the recipe, cooking it for dinner parties—and, in the case of the late Paula Peck, including a version of it in an excellent cookbook, *The Art of Good Cooking*, (1961).

In the same year, Julia Child, Simone Beck, and Louisette Bertholle's watershed book, *Mastering the Art of French Cooking*, Volume One, appeared with its recipe for mashed potatoes cooked with two entire heads of garlic. Of course, both Beard and Child were reporting a technique that some regions of France had utilized for ages. The Greeks, too, had traditionally used garlic as a vegetable, and many other cultures seasoned their food liberally with garlic and had been doing so for many generations.

But it took James Beard and his famous chicken recipe to raise America's garlic consciousness. Garlic as a delicate, buttery-tender vegetable or major ingredient was something totally unexpected. Cooks brave enough to try it and diners brave enough to taste it were astonished at the unctuous texture and the mild, mouthfilling, comforting taste. (In fact, the taste was so different from garlic's usual pungency that many diners didn't know they were eating garlic until they were told.) While word of Beard's chicken and Child's mashed potatoes percolated through America's growing constituency of food enthusiasts, a young American, Lloyd J. Harris, was developing an obsession that would eventually bring about the American garlic revolution in earnest. Lloyd J. Harris's obsession exploded on the country in the form of a book, *The Book of Garlic*, in 1974, and an organization, Lovers of the Stinking Rose, formed in the same year. With tireless devotion, Harris has thrown himself into the garlic cause by lauding its medicinal benefits with great seriousness, its occult benefits with tongue firmly in cheek, and its culinary benefits with unadulterated glee.

In 1971, in Berkeley, California, Alice Waters opened the now-famous restaurant, Chez Panisse. Her love of Southern French cuisine, her devotion to the freshest and best of locally grown ingredients, and her talent—along with that of her chefs—are directly responsible for that engulfing and exciting phenomenon, "New American Cuisine." Harris convinced Waters to stage a Garlic Festival beginning on Bastille Day, 1976. This epic weeklong celebration became an annual event. Eventually, through Harris's efforts, what began with Chez Panisse encompassed the entire city of Berkeley; now Chez Panisse is but one of many participants in the Berkeley Garlic Festival. Other cities and restaurants have followed suit; on July 10, 1983, Mayor Bradley proclaimed Los Angeles Garlic Week; a Washington state restaurant, The Ark, holds an annual festival.

The final stage of the total garlicking of America began quietly in an agricultural community in California's Santa Clara Valley, in a town once known as "Home of the Prune." Prunes lack glamour and romance. Gilroy, California, was sitting on a gold mine of garlic (90 per cent of U.S. garlic production is grown in the Gilroy area) and ignoring it for the wrinkled, faintly ridiculous prune. But in 1978, the Gilroy Rotary Club, along with some garlic growers, threw a garlic-theme luncheon featuring all manner of garlic dishes. The purpose of the luncheon was to promote Gilroy's *fresh* garlic industry. (Much of the garlic grown at that time was processed into garlic salt, powder, and flakes.) A number of food journalists were invited to attend the luncheon which was a huge success. The enthusiasm of the food writers, and the recently acquired knowledge of an annual festival in the garlic-growing town of Arleux, France set wheels turning. A garlic festival—why not? The rest is history. The Gilroy Garlic Festival has become an American phenomenon. Suddenly garlic is in the air, literally and figuratively, and those who despise that allium breeze are fewer and fewer each year.

Buying, Storing, and Using Garlic

There are several varieties of garlic, but those found in most American markets are the purplish-red and the white. Choose fresh garlic carefully. Try to avoid garlic packaged in boxes; you need to be able to lift the bulbs in your hand and squeeze them. Buy large, heavy bulbs that have not begun to sprout and have no shriveled or bruised cloves. (Remember, a clove is one section and a bulb or head is the whole thing.) If only small heads are available, increase the amount of garlic used in each recipe. Keep the garlic heads in a basket in a cool, well-ventilated part of the kitchen. Do not refrigerate them.

Don't buy too much garlic at a time. As it loses its freshness, it begins to shrivel and sprout. Never use shriveled cloves or those that develop bad spots. If the cloves are firm but have begun to sprout, do not use them whole in long-cooked, mild dishes. They may still be crushed or minced, however, and used as a seasoning. Split each sprouting clove, remove and discard the green sprout, and proceed.

Fresh garlic kept in a dry, well-ventilated place will last about a month. If it is necessary to store garlic longer, peel the cloves, cover them with olive oil, and store them in the refrigerator, where they will keep for three months.

To store garlic conveniently for any length of time without the use of oil, Madelene Hill from Hilltop Herb Farm in Texas suggests using the freezer. Her advice: "Buy only the freshest heads. Separate the heads into cloves (no need to peel) and place in plastic bags. Tie the bags closed and freeze. The garlic will keep indefinitely in the freezer, and your freezer will *not* smell like garlic. To use, simply remove as many cloves as you need, peel while still frozen, and use as you would unfrozen garlic."

Braids of garlic are very attractive and an ornament to any kitchen, but in many parts of the country they may be far from fresh. If the heads contain some shriveled cloves, use the braids for decoration and buy your cooking garlic loose. If you live in a garlic-growing area and can purchase fresh braids, use the bulbs quickly.

UTENSILS Serious garlic lovers should have on hand the following equipment:

A sharp knife and a wooden chopping board for mincing and chopping garlic cloves. Keep the wooden board well scrubbed to prevent bacteria and odor. Keep the knife sharpened.

9

A rubber mallet for crushing. Using this utensil for whacking garlic cloves gives the cook a marvelous sense of release. It is almost as good a tension reliever as kneading bread dough.

A fine-meshed sieve or strainer and a "pusher" (a wooden pestle, spatula, or spoon). You will use this time and time again for straining soups and sauces containing whole, long-cooked garlic cloves. Pushing them through the mesh reduces them to a purée. If they were cooked unpeeled, the skin stays behind as the pulp goes through.

A perforated pottery "garlic crock" or a loosely woven wire basket to store the bulbs.

A few "nonreactive" pots—pots that will not chemically react with acid ingredients such as wine, citrus juices, or tomatoes, causing the color or flavor of food to turn. Stainless steel, glass, ceramics, and enamel are nonreactive materials, while copper, cast iron, and aluminum are considered "reactive."

GARLIC HINTS Don't forget that the old way of using garlic as a pungent seasoning is still wonderful. Some hints follow to help you season splendidly.

In its raw form, garlic is powerful. Those misguided souls who persist in thinking of garlic as vulgar, and even inedible, are usually thinking about it in its raw state. Pungency can be tempered by marinating raw garlic in an acid solution, using citrus juice, vinegar, or wine. But remember that raw garlic has an excitement all its own. It may not do as an everyday food, but it provides an occasional exhilarating jolt to jaded taste buds.

Avoid garlic presses. They will reduce garlic to an evil-smelling mush. Instead mince the cloves with a sharp knife, or—for maximum garlickly flavor—crush them by whacking them with a rubber mallet (available in all hardware stores). Crushing raw garlic releases its oils and the flavor will be at its strongest. The mallet method has the added advantage of facilitating the peeling. Hit the unpeeled clove lightly with the mallet to loosen the skin, remove the skin, and then hit the clove several times to crush it. No mallet? Until you get one, use the flat side of a chef's knife or cleaver to press down on the clove. Then remove the loosened skin and proceed.

Raw garlic, if allowed to sauté until brown, becomes bitter, unpleasant, and indigestible. Instead, sauté it very gently and, at the very most, allow it to turn a very pale golden color. *Do not* let it brown, or the dish will be spoiled. However, whole garlic cloves that have been gentled by simmering or boiling can be browned and even caramelized with delicious results.

Garlic powder, garlic salt, and granulated garlic impart an acrid, rancid flavor to foods. Avoid these products by using fresh cloves instead.

A salad without garlic is like a hug without a kiss, a day without sunshine; in fact, it's a damn shame. One of the best ways to permeate a salad with the flavor of garlic is to split a clove, then rub the salad bowl thoroughly with the split clove. Let the bowl dry for a few moments, then add the salad ingredients, the dressing, and toss. Add an additional scent of garlic by rubbing the heel of a stale loaf of French bread thoroughly with a split clove. Toss this *chapon* in with the salad.

Whoever gets to eat the crunchy, flavorful morsel is very lucky indeed.

If you want to add garlic flavor to a sauce or sauté, but want no actual garlic pieces in the finished dish, put some cloves of garlic on toothpicks. Sauté them, simmer them, and then—before the dish is served—pluck them out by their toothpicks. They make a perfectly delicious little treat for the cook.

If you want to add zest to your favorite fried chicken recipe, try Andrea Smith's method. Andrea, an Atlanta cooking teacher and food consultant, recalls her mother's secret of delicious fried chicken: "the use of garlic and onions to flavor the frying oil." Heat oil, add sliced onion and chopped garlic and cook until golden. Discard solids and proceed with your recipe. This works well for frying fish and shellfish as well.

A FEW WORDS ON INGREDIENTS

Butter. Nothing compares with the taste of sweet, unsalted butter. Do not use salted butter, whipped butter, or margarine for the recipes in this book. To clarify butter, heat it slowly in a heavy pan. Skim off the foam and let the sediment settle on the bottom of the pan. Slowly pour the butter through a strainer that is lined with several thicknesses of cheesecloth, discarding the sediment. The clarified butter will keep in the refrigerator for months.

Cheeses. Buy the best available. Do *not* substitute Danish Fontina for the superior Italian kind, for instance, if you can possibly help it. Never use those horrible gluey triangles of processed cheese, misguidedly labeled Gruyère, in place of the real thing from Switzer-

land. And avoid those dreadful jars of domestic sawdust passed off as Parmesan. More and more supermarkets across the country are carrying quality cheeses these days, and many cities and towns have excellent cheese shops. Use them well. Your cooking will suffer if you settle for inferior cheeses.

Stock. Many of the recipes call for stock. It is easy to make your own and store it in the freezer, but should you have none on hand, there are various canned broths available. For best results, buy a broth that does not need diluting. Avoid bouillon cubes.

Herbs. Fresh herbs are the ideal, of course, but they are not always obtainable. If you must use dried herbs, buy them in small quantity, store them in a cool, dark, dry place (*not* on a shelf above the stove), and throw them away if they start to lose their fragrance and grow musty. The rule of thumb is to use three times as much fresh herb as dried, but be careful: too much dried herb in a dish can be disastrous. When using dried herbs, crumble them between your fingers to release the flavor before dropping them into the pot. Dried herbs are best added toward the beginning of the cooking process, fresh toward the end.

Salt. The desirable amount of salt is very much a matter of taste, so please your own taste. I believe less is better for both palatability and health. Too much salt will mask the delicate play of garlic and seasonings in most dishes. You will find, on the whole, that you need much less salt than usual in these particular recipes; the garlic, whether mild or pungent, provides a lot of flavor.

Pepper. Keep a pepper mill by the stove,

and use it. Preground pepper is just sharp, black dust; its flavor does not compare with the freshly ground.

Bay Leaves. Two kinds are available on your grocery shelves: Turkish and California. If a recipe calls for a bay leaf, use a whole Turkish leaf or half of the much stronger California one.

GARLIC AS A GENTLE VEGETABLE Each recipe in this book is rated from mild to pungent and indicated by 1 to 3 garlic heads to make it clear what effect garlic has in each dish.

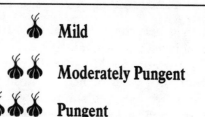

Think of garlic as more than seasoning. It can be at its best and most interesting when used by the handful. Long, gentle cooking renders the cloves sweet, mild, and utterly surprising.

Basic Recipes and Sauces

"It may or not help when you frolic,
  Or cure you of cancer or colic,
  But it sure is delicious
  When you add to your dishes
  Very large doses of garlic."
                      STEPHEN KREITZMAN

ROASTED GARLIC

Roasting whole garlic produces a spectacular first course. The purée, spread on buttered, toasted rounds of French bread, is a revelation; the taste is intense, yet mild and utterly delicious. Roasted garlic also serves as a first step in making garlic purée for use as an ingredient in other recipes.

If served as a first course, reassure guests as you bring the dish—a whole head of garlic on a dinner plate can be frightening to the uninitiated. Demonstrate the proper method of spreading the softened cloves on buttered toast.

Whole heads of garlic
Toasted rounds of French bread
Softened sweet butter

1. Preheat oven to 375° F.

2. Remove the papery outer covering of whole garlic heads, but do not separate the cloves or peel them. Place as many whole heads of garlic on a large square of heavy-duty aluminum foil as there are people to be served. Fold up the foil so that the cloves are completely wrapped.

3. Bake in the preheated oven for 1 hour 15 minutes.

4. Serve each diner a head of garlic and some bread and butter. Separate the cloves. Hold a clove over a piece of buttered bread and squeeze. The garlic purée will pop out, like toothpaste from a tube.

GARLIC PUREE

Keep a supply of this lovely stuff in the refrigerator at all times, and use it to liven up all kinds of dishes. Stir it into soups and stews by the spoonful; heat it in melted butter and pour over steaks and fish; combine with scrambled eggs and grated cheese; use it to thicken sauces; and spread it on bread. Garlic popcorn—freshly popped popcorn tossed with hot butter and a dollop of garlic purée—makes a simple, unbelievably savory snack. Use no salt; the garlic flavor is all you need.

1. To make a batch of garlic purée for later use, let roasted heads of garlic (preceding recipe) cool, unwrapped, for at least 5 minutes.

2. Gently separate the cloves and squeeze each one over a fine-meshed sieve, so that the softened garlic pops into the sieve.

3. With a wooden spatula or spoon, rub the garlic through the sieve into a small container or bowl.

4. Cover tightly with plastic wrap and refrigerate until the purée is needed.

QUICK PURÉE If you are in a hurry, you may skip the refinement of the sieve. Simply squeeze the cloves, one by one, over a bowl. When they have all been squeezed, use a rubber spatula to push the purée into a neat mound, cover tightly with plastic wrap, and refrigerate until needed. It will keep for months. To keep indefinitely, cover with a film of olive oil.

BARBECUED GARLIC

This version of roasted garlic is from the Fresh Garlic Association. Serve it with grilled meat and cooked vegetables and squeeze the garlic onto the meat and vegetables as you eat them. This is ambrosial with hamburgers and corn on the cob; steak and grilled eggplant halves; grilled, butterflied, marinated leg of lamb and tiny green beans; or even hot dogs and baked beans!

8 heads garlic
4 tablespoons butter
A few sprigs fresh rosemary or oregano

1. Place whole heads of garlic, prepared as for Roasted Garlic, on a sheet of heavy-duty foil.

2. Top with butter (4 tablespoons for 8 heads) and a few sprigs of fresh rosemary or oregano. If fresh herbs are unavailable, substitute dried (2 teaspoons of dried herb for 8 heads of garlic). Fold the foil over the garlic and seal the package well.

3. Cook over hot coals for about 45 minutes, turning the package occasionally with tongs.

SIMMERED GARLIC CLOVES

Another method of handling garlic turns the cloves into tender morsels with a sweet, faintly nutty flavor. They are sensational tossed into buttered pasta, baked in a quiche, or simmered in a soup.

Garlic cloves
Stock or water
Olive oil

1. Separate any number of garlic cloves. Place in a saucepan with enough boiling water to just cover. Boil for 3 minutes. Drain, rinse under cold running water, and peel (the skins will slip right off).

2. Return the garlic to the saucepan. Cover generously with stock or water. Bring to a simmer and gently cook for 15 minutes, or until the cloves are very tender.

3. Drain (if you used stock, save it for another use; it will be very flavorful) and store the cloves in a well-covered bowl or jar in the refrigerator until needed. They will keep for several days. To store for a greater length of time, cover with olive oil.

SAUTEED GARLIC CLOVES

This is a variation on the simmered cloves. It can be stored in the refrigerator for weeks.

Garlic cloves
Unsalted butter

1. Boil the garlic cloves for 2 to 3 minutes. Drain, rinse under cold water, and peel.

2. Melt butter in a heavy skillet. Cook the cloves gently in the butter for 15 minutes.

3. Mash the cloves and use them in a sauce or toss them whole, butter and all, into pasta, rice, or a cracked wheat pilaf.

GARLIC AS A THICKENING AND FLAVORING AGENT

🧄 The garlic will thicken the sauce as well as imbue it with a gently mysterious quality, unidentifiable as garlic, but ravishingly delicious.

1. Toss unpeeled cloves (the more the merrier) into the pot with the other ingredients when making a meat stew or roast or a chicken sauté. Cook in the usual manner.

2. When done, remove meat or chicken and keep warm.

3. Degrease the pan juices.

4. Strain the pan juices and garlic through a fine-meshed sieve, pushing down on the garlic cloves so that the pulp rubs through but the skins remain behind.

5. Recombine meat or poultry with the garlic-enriched sauce, reheat briefly and serve.

GARLIC AND OLIVE OIL PASTE

🧄🧄🧄 While the previous recipes give you a taste of garlic as a vegetable, these show it in its more traditional guise, as an assertive seasoning. This makes a strong and versatile garlic–olive oil paste that will keep indefinitely in the refrigerator. Use it for salad dressings, spreading on crusty bread, tossing with pasta, rubbing on chicken before roasting, etc.

Makes about 1 quart

4 to 5 heads garlic
1 quart olive oil

1. Add 4 to 5 heads of garlic (separate the cloves, hit them lightly with a rubber mallet or cleaver, and peel them) to 1 quart of olive oil.

2. Let the garlic marinate for a week.

3. Using a food processor, now make the cloves and oil into a paste.

4. Store the mixture in a jar or bottle in the refrigerator.

CHRISTIANE'S AIOLI

♣♣♣ From Christiane Lauterbach, a talented French home cook, here is the recipe for the classic "butter of Provence" and her description of how it is served.

"Aïoli is a garlic mayonnaise. It is also the name of the Provençal 'boiled dinner,' traditionally served with a young red wine. It can be as simple as a piece of salt cod, freshened and poached, and some potatoes boiled in their skins. It can be a feast with new artichokes, string beans, asparagus, finocchio (fennel), hard-cooked eggs, small squid, periwinkles, snails, in addition to the customary cod and potatoes.

The sauce is best made with a mortar and pestle. All ingredients must be at room temperature. The quantity of oil you will be able to incorporate into the sauce will vary with your level of skill and the weather."

Makes about 2 cups

10 large cloves of garlic, peeled, sprout (if any) removed
2 egg yolks
Pinch of salt
1¼–2 cups virgin olive oil
Juice of 1 lemon
Salt and freshly ground pepper to taste

1. Pound the garlic in the mortar until reduced to a smooth paste.

2. Add the egg yolks and a pinch of salt. Beat with your pestle or a wooden spoon until the eggs are pale yellow.

3. Dribble in the oil drop by drop at the beginning, a bit faster as the sauce thickens, *stirring constantly* with the pestle or wooden spoon. Any time the sauce gets too thick add ¼ teaspoon of lemon juice. Be careful at the end; if the weather is hot, the egg yolks may not absorb the full amount of oil.

4. Season to taste with salt and freshly ground pepper.

"Aïoli gently intoxicates, charges the body with warmth, bathes the soul with rapture. In its essence, it concentrates the force and the joy of the sun of Provence. Around an aïoli, well perfumed and bright as a vein of gold, where are there men who would not recognize themselves as brothers?"
FRÉDÉRIC MISTRAL

GARLIC BÉCHAMEL

🧄🧄🧄 The garlic purée gives this basic white sauce a mysterious and special new dimension. It is an ingredient in several of the recipes in this book, but it can be used anywhere a white sauce would be used. Mundane macaroni and cheese, for instance, becomes a unique dish when made with garlic béchamel.

Makes about 2¾ cups

4 tablespoons unsalted butter
4 tablespoons flour
2½ cups scalded milk (more or less, depending on the thickness of sauce desired)
Salt and freshly ground white pepper to taste
Garlic purée from 3 large heads of Roasted Garlic (see page 14)
1 egg, at room temperature

1. Melt the butter in a heavy saucepan and whisk in the flour. Let this *roux* cook over low heat, stirring constantly, for 3 to 4 minutes.

2. Whisk in the scalded milk. Bring to a boil. Reduce the heat and cook gently, stirring frequently, for 10 to 15 minutes. Add salt and pepper and whisk in the garlic purée. Remove from the heat.

3. Beat the egg in a bowl. Beat some of the sauce into the egg. Next beat the egg mixture back into the garlic sauce. Taste and correct seasonings.

4. Store in the refrigerator, with plastic wrap directly on the surface of the sauce, until needed. Thin with milk before using if necessary.

> "Seasoners are the poetry of food, and its music too.... What is garlic? The tuba."
> **WAVERLY ROOT**
> *Herbs and Spices,* 1980

GARLIC BEARNAISE SAUCE

🧄 This is a classic sauce—a rich creamy emulsion of egg yolks and butter—that has been given a garlic accent. It is absolutely wonderful with beef, from the haughty filet to the lowly hamburger, and it's pretty good with vegetables, too: steamed asparagus, green beans, or new potatoes in particular.

Watch the heat of the butter. If the sauce exceeds 140 degrees, it will separate, eggs on the bottom, butter on top. Should it exceed 175 degrees, the eggs will scramble and you will end up with a mess. Use an instant-read thermometer if you are unsure of yourself. For a more pungent taste, chop some parsley and raw garlic together and stir it into the sauce just before serving.

Makes about 2 cups

½ cup white wine (use Rapazzini's garlic wine if you can find it)
⅓ cup tarragon wine vinegar
3 cloves garlic, crushed
2 tablespoons minced shallots
½ teaspoon dried tarragon
1 tablespoon chopped fresh parsley
Salt and freshly ground pepper to taste
3 egg yolks, at room temperature
1 cup clarified butter, melted, warm *not* hot

1. Combine all the ingredients except the egg yolks and butter in a saucepan. Bring to a boil, reduce the heat, and simmer briskly until almost all the liquid has evaporated. Cool thoroughly.

2. Place the cooled garlic mixture and the egg yolks in a large, heavy saucepan over low heat. Use an asbestos pad or flame tamer under the pot. Whisk the yolks quickly and vigorously. As they begin to poach, they will turn frothy, custardy, and thick. Watch your heat. After 3 or 4 minutes, remove the pot from the heat.

3. Immediately begin whisking in the warm (not hot) butter—driblet by driblet. Keep whisking hard and fast. If the butter is not too hot and you whisk constantly, the egg yolks will expand as they absorb the butter, and the sauce will be lovely, creamy, and thick. Do not make this sauce more than an hour or so ahead of time and do not reheat it.

PESTO

🧄🧄🧄 Pesto is a vivid, earthy classic. For a gorgeous (visually as well as gastronomically) summer first course, fill lightly poached mushroom caps with the bright green pesto, arrange on sliced juicy, ripe tomatoes, and garnish with whole basil leaves. To store the sauce, refrigerate with a film of olive oil on its surface. It will keep for weeks.

Makes about 1½ cups

4–5 cups fresh basil leaves
5 tablespoons parsley leaves
4 cloves garlic
¼ cup pine nuts
Salt and freshly ground pepper to taste
¾ cup olive oil
¾ cup grated Parmesan cheese

1. Place the basil, parsley, garlic, pine nuts, salt and pepper, olive oil, and ½ cup of the grated Parmesan in a blender jar. Blend to a rough, coarse paste.

2. Scrape the paste into a bowl. Stir in the ¼ cup additional grated cheese.

3. To serve, toss with hot linguine or fettucine, stir into summer vegetable soups, fold into omelets, or spoon onto cooked fish.

GARLIC BREATH

Long after the last morsel of a garlic-laden dish is gone, the memory lingers on in every breath. This is true, even if the dish tasted mild and sweet. Different people seem to have different susceptibility to garlic breath. There are many remedies bandied about for this age-old problem, but, alas, they do not work. Breath mints and mouthwashes do no good at all; the problem is not in the mouth but in the lungs and in the very pores of the skin.

Many people recommend large quantities of parsley—either cooked with the garlic or chewed after the meal. A French person might recommend munching on coffee beans or anise seeds, and a Greek might suggest downing a shot of spirits or even swallowing a raw garlic clove *before* the garlic meal. Ford Maddox Ford, in a famous excerpt from *Provence*, claims garlic breath "attends only those timorous creatures who have not the courage as it were to wallow in that vegetable." An erroneous conclusion. If you wallow in garlic, you will smell of it. And all the parsley, coffee beans, and spirits in the world will not help.

There is a bright side to this whole problem. If the cloves eaten were long-cooked and mellow, the subsequent garlic odor will be mellow, too. And if you see that your friends and family eat as much garlic as you do, no one will notice the smell.

GREMOLATA

🧄🧄🧄 *Gremolata* is a strong and bracing raw garlic mixture used in Italian cookery, most notably in a dish of braised veal shanks called *osso buco*. It is very good in all sorts of dishes. Try it in a beef stew, veal stew, or chicken sauté.

This mixture is particularly good for people on a salt-free diet. It adds a big wallop of flavor without a speck of salt. For those on a low-fat or low-calorie diet, leave out the olive oil.

Makes 3–4 tablespoons

1 lemon
3 cloves garlic
Generous handful fresh parsley
2 tablespoons olive oil

1. Peel the lemon, being careful to leave the white pith behind.

2. Chop the lemon rind, garlic, and parsley together until very fine.

3. Place the mixture in a bowl and stir in the olive oil.

4. Add to soups, stews, or sauces for the last 10 minutes or so of cooking time.

GARLIC BARBECUE

🧄 When grilling meats outdoors, throw a few cloves of unpeeled garlic on the coals toward the end of the cooking time. The meat (and the air) will have a lovely smoky hint of garlic. Pork, lamb, or swordfish cubes are particularly delicious cooked in this manner.

1. When making kebabs on thin skewers, alternate the usual cubes of meat, mushroom caps, and pieces of onions and green pepper with parboiled large, whole, unpeeled garlic cloves.

2. Brush the kebabs with a vinaigrette or teriyaki-type marinade and grill over charcoal or wood.

Appetizers and Dips

"Garlic! Thou art the supreme appetizer, the sole condiment, the glorious, the sovereign extract of the earth."

GUSTAVE COQUOIT

GARLIC COEURS A LA CREME

🧄*Coeurs à la crème* are traditionally prepared in small, perforated, heart-shaped molds, available in most cookware shops, but if you do not have molds, note the directions for using a colander. *Coeurs à la crème* are usually sweet, but this version is not. It uses a food I much admire: fresh goat cheese. If you can't find (or don't like) goat cheese, substitute cream cheese. But do try goat—aside from the compelling, tangy taste and creamy texture, the advantage of goat cheese is its low fat and low calorie content (70 calories per ounce as opposed to cream cheese's 106 calories an ounce). If you use Montrachet, scrape off the cover of wood ash (or buy without), otherwise the final mixture will be gray.

Serves 8

1 pound low-fat cottage cheese
1 pound fresh, white goat cheese (Montrachet or Boucheron, preferably)
Purée from 2 heads Roasted Garlic (see pages 14-15)
2 cups plain yogurt

1. Rub the cottage cheese through a sieve into a mixing bowl.

2. With a wooden spoon, or electric mixer, beat the goat cheese and the garlic purée into the cottage cheese. Beat in the yogurt.

3. Line 8 *coeur à la crème* molds with damp cheesecloth, allowing an overhang. Spoon mixture into molds, wrap and place on a rack over a deep plate. Refrigerate overnight to drain.

4. Unwrap and unmold onto 8 small plates. Discard cheesecloth.

5. Serve with thin brown bread, toast, or bagels and slices of smoked salmon, if desired.

SAVORY CREME Lacking *coeur à la crème* molds, spoon the mixture into a cheesecloth-lined colander and refrigerate overnight to drain. Unmold onto a serving platter and allow each diner to scoop off a portion.

GARLIC-STUFFED MUSHROOMS

🧄 The pecans give the stuffing a crunch; the mild garlic sauce gives a hint of mystery; and the cayenne, a touch of tongue-tingling heat. All in all, each mushroom cap is a most satisfying mouthful.

Serves 4-6

12 medium mushrooms
3 tablespoons unsalted butter
2 scallions, sliced
1 ½ tablespoons coarsely ground pecans
1 ½ tablespoons bread crumbs
1 ½ tablespoons freshly grated Parmesan
     cheese
¼ cup Garlic Béchamel (see page 19)
Salt and freshly ground pepper to taste
Cayenne pepper

1. Preheat oven to 450° F.

2. Clean the mushrooms. Remove the stems and reserve.

3. Parboil the mushrooms in just enough water to cover for 3 minutes, until barely cooked. Drain well, blot with paper towels, and set aside until needed.

4. If the tip of the stems seem woody, trim them away. Chop stems coarsely.

5. Melt 2 tablespoons of the butter in a skillet. Toss in the chopped mushroom stems and scallions. Sauté until tender and most of the mushroom juices have evaporated. Toss in the pecans, bread crumbs, Parmesan cheese, and the remaining tablespoon of butter. Stir until the butter is melted and absorbed. Stir in the garlic béchamel. Add salt and freshly ground pepper to taste.

6. Stuff each mushroom cap with the mixture, mounding it neatly over the top. Sprinkle each with some cayenne pepper. Put the stuffed mushrooms in a lightly oiled, shallow baking dish. Bake for 10 minutes or just until heated through.

7. Serve at once.

THE EVIL EYE

As potent as garlic was thought to be against earthly ills, it was considered even more powerful as protection against evil and unpredictable forces. When my husband was born in 1939, one of his great-grandmothers rushed to the hospital brandishing a clove of garlic strung on a ribbon. This was—in Yiddish—a *Kineahora bendl,* a charm to protect the new baby from the evil eye. A Chinese or a Greek great-grandmother might have done the same, while parents in the Middle Ages might have garlanded the cradle with braids of garlic, to prevent mischievous fairies from stealing the baby and substituting a changeling.

PATE WITH GARLIC

🧄 Whole garlic cloves are added to the meat mixture, so that when this pâté is cut, the pieces of white garlic look like the bits of pork fat that are often found in pâtés of this type. The texture of the garlic is smooth and unctuous, almost as if it were, indeed, pork fat, but the taste is a mild and happy surprise. For best flavor, serve at room temperature. The pâté will keep for 2 weeks in the refrigerator.

Makes 3½ pounds pâté

1½ pounds ground pork shoulder, fat and lean
½ pound ground veal
1 pound ground beef chuck
1 large onion, minced
2 tablespoons unsalted butter
½ cup bread crumbs
2 eggs, lightly beaten
¼ cup Cognac
Salt and freshly ground pepper to taste
2 tablespoons chopped parsley
¼ teaspoon nutmeg
½ teaspoon dried thyme
¼ teaspoon allspice
½ teaspoon dry mustard
1 teaspoon marjoram
1 teaspoon anise seeds
¼ teaspoon mace
½ cup unsalted pistachios, shelled
30 large cloves garlic, boiled for 3 minutes, peeled and simmered in water to cover for 15 minutes
½ pound bacon, sliced

1. Preheat oven to 350° F.

2. Place the ground meats in a bowl.

3. Sauté the onion in butter until tender. Add to the meats.

4. Add crumbs, eggs, Cognac, and all seasonings. Add the pistachios and whole garlic cloves. Use your hands to mix together very well. Fry a tiny piece in a skillet and taste; adjust seasonings to your liking. This pâté should have a lively flavor. Remember that chilling will mute the seasonings a bit.

5. Line a 2-quart loaf pan with bacon strips, letting them extend up the sides of the pan and over the edge. Fill the pan with the meat mixture, pressing it down to even it out and eliminate air spaces. Fold the overhanging bacon over the meat, adding more strips, as necessary, to cover the top.

6. Place the loaf pan in a wide, shallow pan. Pour in 2 inches of boiling water. Place in the preheated oven and bake for about 1½ hours, until the juices run clear, and an instant-read thermometer registers 170 degrees.

7. Pour off the fat and juices into a jar. Refrigerate the jar. Let the pâté rest for 15 minutes. Then cover the pâté with foil. Top with a brick or two or with a cutting board weighted with heavy cans. Refrigerate overnight, weights and all. Next day, remove the weights; then remove the pâté from the loaf pan and discard any solidified fat. Do not disturb the bacon strips. Wrap the pâté in plastic wrap or foil. Refrigerate for 2 to 3 days before serving so that flavors develop.

8. Scrape off the solidified fat from the meat juices in the jar and discard the fat. Save the delicious jellied juices to serve with the pâté, if desired, or use it to enrich soups and stews.

9. Serve the pâté in thin slices with Onion-Garlic Relish (see page 29), if desired.

> **"Garlic is one of the most gracious gifts of gods to men—a gift, alas! all too frequently abused. Brazen, and crude, and screaming, when dragged into undue prominence, it may yet be made to harmonize divinely with fish and fowl, with meat and other greens."**
> ELIZABETH ROBBINS PENNELL
> *The Delights of Delicate Eating,* 1901

SCALLOP CEVICHE

The scallops are not subjected to direct heat, but they are "cooked" by the action of the lime juice. The pungent taste is not all garlic; the chilies do their part, too.

Serves 4

1 pound fresh sea scallops, quartered
1 cup fresh lime juice
3 small green chilies, chopped
2 cloves garlic, minced
2 tablespoons chopped parsley
½ cup chopped sweet onion
Salt and freshly ground pepper to taste
Lettuce leaves
Chopped fresh coriander (Chinese parsley)

1. Combine all ingredients except the coriander and lettuce. Allow the scallops to marinate overnight in the refrigerator.

2. Line 4 clear glass goblets with lettuce leaves. Spoon ¼ of scallop mixture into each goblet. Sprinkle with coriander and serve.

EGGPLANT IN GARLIC SAUCE ORIENTALE

🧄🧄 When tiny Oriental eggplants are available, Fournou's Ovens, a restaurant in San Francisco, will prepare this special first course if it is ordered in advance. Many supermarkets across the country carry these eggplants. They also can be found in many Oriental food stores. This recipe can be made in a wok or a skillet. Both the plum sauce and the chili paste are available in Oriental groceries.

Serves 6

4 small Chinese eggplants (each about 6 inches long)
2 tablespoons peanut oil
3 tablespoons sherry
2 tablespoons soy sauce
1¼ cups chicken stock
3 tablespoons finely minced garlic
1 tablespoon finely minced fresh ginger
½ cup plum sauce
2 teaspoons hot chili paste
2 teaspoons sugar
2 tablespoons cornstarch mixed with enough chicken stock to form paste

1. Remove the bud ends and slice the eggplants in half lengthwise. Then cut the eggplant into ¾-inch-square cubes, as evenly as possible.

2. Heat 1½ tablespoons of the oil in a wok. Add eggplant and stir-fry rapidly until almost tender, about 5 minutes.

3. Deglaze the pan with the sherry and soy sauce. Moisten with about ½ cup of the chicken stock and reduce by half by rapid boiling. Remove the eggplant and set aside.

4. Clean wok with paper towels. Put the remaining ½ tablespoon oil in the wok and add the garlic and ginger, stir-frying rapidly and constantly.

5. After several seconds, add the plum sauce, chili paste, and sugar. Add about ½ cup of the remaining chicken stock and reduce by one third.

6. Return the eggplant cubes to the wok containing the sauce mixture. Stir-fry quickly to heat through.

7. Add the remaining ¼ cup chicken stock. Stir in some of the cornstarch paste. Stir and cook until the sauce is thick enough to coat a spoon. Add the entire mixture if necessary.

8. Place on a heated platter and serve immediately.

ONION-GARLIC RELISH

Serve this sweet-and-sour relish as part of an assortment of hors d'oeuvres or as an accompaniment to pâtés.

Makes about 1 ½ cups

½ cup raisins
½ cup dark rum
3 tablespoons olive oil
1 ¼ pounds pearl onions, parboiled and peeled
60 cloves garlic, parboiled and peeled
1 tablespoon sugar
¼ cup chicken stock or water
6 large, ripe tomatoes, peeled, seeded, juiced, and chopped (substitute canned when good tomatoes are out of season)
Salt and freshly ground pepper to taste

THE GARLIC TIMES

There is a newsletter specifically for garlic lovers, *The Garlic Times*, published by Lloyd J. Harris and his organization, Lovers of the Stinking Rose. LSR's motto is "Fight Mouthwash, Eat Garlic," and they laud the garlic cause with great gusto in every issue. Where else would one find a "Mail Odor" page offering garlic posters, garlic buttons, garlic bumper stickers and T-shirts, even garlic jewelry?

1. Combine the raisins and rum in a small bowl. Let raisins marinate while you prepare the onions and garlic.

2. Heat the oil in a wide, heavy nonreactive skillet. Spread the onions and garlic in the skillet and sauté, shaking the pan so that they are evenly tossed in the hot oil for a few minutes.

3. Sprinkle the onions and garlic with the sugar and continue to cook over moderate heat, shaking the pan frequently to ensure even browning.

4. When the onions and garlic have caramelized and turned a deep amber brown, pour in the stock or water to dissolve the caramelized bits adhering to the skillet. Shake and cook until the liquid is almost gone and the onions and garlic are deeply and evenly browned.

5. Stir in the tomatoes and season with salt and pepper. Stir in the raisins and their soaking rum.

6. Bring to a simmer and cook, covered, for 30 to 40 minutes, until the mixture is very thick and the onions and garlic are very tender. During the simmering time, uncover to stir occasionally.

7. Allow the mixture to cool, then refrigerate overnight so that flavors can develop. Serve at room temperature.

AJADA (POTATO AND GARLIC DIP)

♣♣♣ This is a Sephardic Jewish recipe, a close relative of the Greek potato-garlic sauce known as *skordalia*.

Makes about 5 ½ cups

4 Idaho potatoes
3 cloves garlic, crushed
Juice of 3 lemons
2 eggs
Salt to taste
¼ cup olive oil

1. Peel the potatoes and boil until tender. Drain.

2. Put the potatoes through a ricer.

3. In an electric mixer, or with a wooden spoon, beat in crushed garlic, lemon juice, eggs, salt, and oil gradually. eat until slightly thicker than mayonnaise.

4. Chill and serve with matzoh or other crackers.

BAGNA CAUDA

♣♣ This garlicky Italian "hot bath" is the sauce for a sort of bread and vegetable fondue. It may also be used as a sauce over steamed vegetables or a dipping sauce for steamed artichokes. It must be kept warm, not boiling hot, so that the butter does not brown and the garlic does not burn and turn bitter.

Makes about 1 cup

¼ pound unsalted butter
½ cup olive oil
6 cloves garlic, peeled and crushed (or more to taste)
1 2-ounce can anchovy fillets

1. Heat the butter and oil until warm. Stir in the garlic. Cook over lowest possible heat for about 5 minutes, stirring occasionally. The garlic must not brown.

2. Stir in the anchovies. Continue to cook,

30

stirring, until the anchovies have disintegrated.

3. Bring to the table in a shallow earthenware pot, and keep warm over a candle warmer. Offer a selection of raw vegetable *crûdités* and crusty bread for diners to dip into the sauce.

SIDNEY'S AVOCADO DIP

An Atlanta restaurant, Sidney's Just South, serves this with raw vegetables as a salad course. Don't make it too long before serving or it will lose its bright green color.

Makes about 3 cups

2 large ripe avocados
1 lime
2 cloves garlic, crushed
Salt and freshly ground pepper to taste
3 tablespoons olive oil
3 tablespoons jalapeño relish (available in cans at the supermarket in the Mexican or ethnic food section)
¾ cup sour cream

1. Cut the avocados in half and remove the pits. Scoop out the flesh into a bowl.

2. Mash the avocado flesh with lime juice, garlic, salt and pepper, olive oil, and jalapeño relish. Mix well.

3. Add sour cream and mix until creamy but not too smooth.

4. Serve at once with romaine leaves, tomato wedges, and slices of cucumber, zucchini, carrots, and bell peppers.

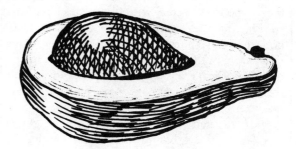

HUMMUS

🧄🧄🧄 "Too much lemon juice," murmured a Lebanese woman who tasted my *hummus* at a food demonstration; "Not enough lemon juice," murmured another simultaneously—which proves that there are as many ways of making this dish as there are Middle Eastern cooks. But they *never* murmur "Too much garlic." In fact, one cook I know uses seven large cloves in her *hummus*. Feel free to add as much garlic as you like.

THE GARLIC CONSORTIUM

Placitas, New Mexico, harbors a lively and enthusiastic band of garlic lovers. Formed in 1979, the Placitas Garlic Consortium is made up of garlic growers, artists, potters (who craft vessels for the storing of the bulbs), and those who love to cook with quantities of garlic. In Placitas, the altitude is about 6,000 feet; both the native purple garlic and the Taos white that thrive in this heady atmosphere were introduced to the area by the Conquistadors. The consortium produces an exquisite garlic oil made from almond oil that is steeped with garlic and then filtered. Placitas purple garlic has one major advantage over its California counterpart: the cloves snap out of their skins like peas from a pod.

Makes about 3 cups

2 cans (15½ ounces each) chick peas
¼ of the liquid from 1 can of chick peas
6 tablespoons tahini (sesame seed paste, available in shops specializing in Middle Eastern foods and many supermarkets, especially those with an ethnic food section)
⅓ cup lemon juice or more to taste
3 large cloves garlic (or more)
Salt and freshly ground pepper to taste
Olive oil, paprika, and chopped parsley for garnish

1. Combine all ingredients, except garnish, in a blender or food processor container. Blend to a smooth, creamy paste. Taste and add more lemon juice or salt to suit your taste. It should be the creamy consistency of mashed potatoes. Thin with chick pea liquid or water if necessary.

2. Scrape into an attractive bowl. Color olive oil with a bit of paprika. Drizzle oil over the surface in a decorative pattern and sprinkle with parsley.

3. Serve with wedges of pita bread and raw vegetables.

TZATZIKI

🧄🧄🧄 *Tzatziki* is a Greek cucumber-yogurt mixture that may be prepared as a dip or a sauce. Salting the cucumbers rids them of wateriness and bitterness.

Makes about 1 ½ cups

2 cups plain yogurt
2 large cucumbers
Salt to taste
2 large cloves garlic, minced
1 ½ teaspoons white wine vinegar
1 tablespoon olive oil
Freshly ground pepper to taste

1. Line a sieve with a damp cheesecloth and place over a large bowl. Dump the yogurt into the sieve, cover with plastic wrap, and allow to drain in the refrigerator for 24 hours.

2. Peel the cucumbers. Cut them in half lengthwise. Using a teaspoon, scrape out and discard the seeds. Grate the cucumbers into a colander, using the large holes on a four-sided grater. Salt the cucumbers and allow them to drain for ½ hour.

3. Place the garlic, vinegar, and olive oil in a bowl and marinate while the cucumbers are draining.

4. Squeeze the drained cucumbers as dry as possible and blot on paper towels. Place in the bowl with the marinated garlic. Add the drained yogurt and stir. Add a few grindings of fresh pepper, and salt, if necessary.

5. Serve with toasted pita bread triangles.

TZATZIKI SAUCE Drain the yogurt for 6 to 7 hours only. The mixture can be used in several ways. It is zesty on hamburger sandwiches. Top each burger with a slice of ripe tomato, a small heap of coarsely grated cabbage, and a dollop of *tzatziki* sauce. It can also be served with grilled meats. The meat juices mingling with the *tzatziki* are utterly delicious.

As a sauce for tomatoes, it is something special. Cut several ripe tomatoes into sections, cutting from stem to stern, but do not cut all the way through. Open the tomato like a flower. Salt lightly and invert on paper towels to drain for a few minutes. Fill each tomato with some *tzatziki* and garnish with fresh mint.

TONNATO DIP

🧄 Adapted from an Italian sauce used to coat cold, sliced roasted veal, this tuna dip is one of my favorite garlic recipes. Make it days in advance; the flavor improves severalfold day by day. Serve with sliced ripe tomatoes; steamed new potatoes; steamed, peeled fresh asparagus; steamed fresh green beans; as a filling for raw mushroom caps; or as a dip with raw vegetable dippers, toasted pita bread triangles, and crackers.

Makes approximately 2 ¾ cups

10 ½ ounces tuna in water, well drained (a 7-ounce can plus a 3 ½ -ounce can)
1 teaspoon capers
2 cups mayonnaise
Purée from 1 head Roasted Garlic (see pages 14-15)
Salt and freshly ground pepper to taste
1 ½ tablespoons lemon juice

1. Combine all the ingredients in the jar of a blender or food processor. Blend until thick and perfectly smooth. Scrape the mixture into a small bowl and refrigerate. Make it several days before serving. It improves with waiting.

2. Bring to room temperature before serving.

Soups

"Garlic soup is, I suggest, strictly for the initiated. This is for male men and their brazen wives, not omitting their primitive brats.... It is garlic nude and unashamed."

OSCAR A. MENDELSOHN
A Salute to Onions, 1966

GARLIC SOUP

🧄 The combinations of flavors and textures in this soup and its accompanying vegetable-spread toasts are very special indeed.

Serves 6

35 cloves garlic
2 tablespoons olive oil
1 small onion, chopped
1 small green pepper, chopped
1 large can (1 pound 12 ounces) plum tomatoes, undrained and chopped
¼ teaspoon allspice
⅛ teaspoon ground cloves
¼ teaspoon tarragon
Salt and freshly ground pepper to taste
4 cups chicken broth
1 egg yolk
6 slices French bread, toasted

1. Boil the unpeeled garlic cloves for 3 minutes in enough water to cover. Drain and peel.

2. Heat the oil in a deep pot. Cook the onion, green pepper, and garlic for 8 to 10 minutes, until soft but not browned. Stir frequently. Add the tomatoes, spices, and broth. Bring to a boil, reduce heat, and simmer uncovered for 20 minutes.

3. Pour the soup through a sieve into a bowl. With a wooden spoon or spatula press down very hard on the solids to extract all juices. Reserve the solids. Return the strained soup to the pot.

4. Beat the egg yolk in a small bowl. With a whisk gradually beat about ¼ cup soup into the yolk, then gradually add the yolk mixture into the soup, beating constantly. Cook gently for 1 or 2 minutes more. Do not boil or the soup will curdle.

5. Spread the reserved vegetable solids on the toasted French bread slices. Arrange on a dish and serve with the soup.

**"Here pungent garlic meets the eager sight
and whets with savor sharp the appetite."**
IBN AL-MUʿTAZZ
Tenth century

ONION GARLIC SOUP

🧄 A variation on the classic French onion soup, with several kinds of onion and plenty of garlic. The preliminary steaming in the covered pot subdues the garlic, so that it does not become bitter during the subsequent browning process. This soup has an astounding sweetness that far surpasses ordinary onion soup.

Serves 6

4 tablespoons unsalted butter
5 cups thinly sliced onions
4 large leeks, trimmed of green parts, cleaned
    well and thinly sliced
½ cup chopped shallots
15 large cloves garlic, minced
1 tablespoon flour
2 quarts rich chicken stock, brought to a boil
½ cup dry white vermouth
Salt and freshly ground pepper to taste

1. Melt the butter in a deep, heavy pot. Stir the onions, leeks, shallots, and garlic into the hot butter. Cover pot and let steam over very low heat for 15 minutes.

2. Uncover. Raise heat slightly. Cook over moderate heat, stirring occasionally, for 40 to 50 minutes, until the vegetables are a deep amber brown.

3. Sprinkle in the flour and stir over low heat for 3 minutes.

4. Whisk in the boiling stock. Add the vermouth and salt and pepper. Simmer, partially covered, for 40 minutes. Stir occasionally.

5. Skim the surface of the soup. Adjust seasoning. Serve at once, very hot. This soup may be made ahead and refrigerated for a few days.

GARLIC HANDS

Many people (dentists who cook, for instance) worry about garlic odors on their hands. Soap and water often works; if not, try rubbing the hands with lemon juice or a little salt. The Fresh Garlic Association offers an interesting remedy; after handling raw garlic, rub your fingers thoroughly with the bowl of a stainless steel spoon under running water, then wash your hands with soap. The metal neutralizes the garlic, and the lingering odor will be gone.

GARLIC VICHYSSOISE WITH SORREL

🧄 Sorrel—sometimes called sour grass—is a green with a tart, acidic edge and a haunting flavor. If sorrel is unavailable, substitute watercress. The taste will be quite different—peppery rather than tart—but it will still be quite good.

Serves 6

2 tablespoons unsalted butter
1 cup sliced scallions, green and white parts
2 leeks, trimmed, well cleaned and sliced
4 cups clear, fat-free chicken broth
60 cloves garlic, parboiled and peeled
4 baking potatoes, peeled and coarsely diced
Salt and freshly ground pepper to taste
2 cups half-and-half
2 cups sorrel, stemmed, trimmed of tough
    center vein, and finely shredded

1. Heat the butter in a heavy pot. Sauté the scallions and leeks until limp.

2. Add the broth, garlic, potatoes, and salt and pepper. Simmer, covered, until the potatoes are tender. Cool. Skim off fat.

3. Put the potato mixture through a food mill or rub through a sieve. Stir in the half-and-half. Taste and adjust seasonings. Chill.

4. Just before serving, stir in the shredded sorrel. Taste and adjust seasonings once more. Serve in chilled bowls.

"The emotional content of garlic almost equals its culinary value."
    A. E. GROSSER
    Placitas Garlic Consortium,
    New Mexico, 1983

PUREE OF BLACK BEAN SOUP

🧄 This soup is very easy to make and has a very interesting play of flavors. It will keep well; in fact, the flavor improves after a day or so of refrigeration.

Serves 6

2 tablespoons bacon fat
2 medium onions, chopped
1 large carrot, peeled and chopped
2 ribs celery, chopped
Pinch ground cloves
¼ teaspoon allspice
¼ teaspoon cumin
Pinch cayenne pepper (or more to taste)
Salt and freshly ground pepper to taste
5 cups chicken stock
2 cans (16 ounces each) black beans, drained well
Purée from 1 large head garlic (see pages 14-15)
Juice of 1 lemon
Crème Fraîche (see page 57) or sour cream

1. Heat bacon fat in a deep heavy pot. Toss in the chopped vegetables. Cover and allow to steam over low heat for 15 minutes.

2. Uncover. Raise the heat slightly and continue to cook until the vegetables are very tender.

3. Add the seasonings and stir over low heat so that the vegetables are coated with the spices.

4. Add the stock and bring to a boil. Stir in the beans. Simmer, partially covered, for 15 to 20 minutes.

5. Cool slightly. Purée the mixture through a food mill or sieve and return it to the pot.

6. Reheat, and taste and correct seasonings. Stir in the garlic purée and lemon juice. Serve piping hot, with a dollop of cold *crème fraîche* or sour cream.

CAULIFLOWER GARLIC SOUP

This soup is rich, buttery, and creamy, yet it is low in calories (91 per serving). Both the garlic and cauliflower, when cooked gently together, lose their usual powerful flavors. This soup is also delicious cold.

Serves 6

20 cloves garlic, peeled
5 cups chicken stock
8 cups cauliflowerets (1 large head)
Salt and freshly ground white pepper to taste
1 cup half-and-half
Freshly grated nutmeg

1. In a covered soup pot, simmer the garlic cloves in the stock for 20 minutes.

2. Add the cauliflowerets and salt and pepper. Cover and continue simmering until the cauliflower and the garlic are very tender, about ½ hour. Cool.

3. In a blender, purée the soup in batches until smooth and velvety. Return the puréed mixture to the soup pot.

4. Stir in the half-and-half. Taste and adjust seasoning. Bring to a simmer.

5. Ladle into heated soup bowls. Top each serving with a grating of fresh nutmeg.

Seafood

"We remember the fish we ate in Egypt . . . the leeks, the onions, the garlic."

OLD TESTAMENT, NUMBERS 11:15

SPICY MARINATED SHRIMP AND GARLIC

♣ This is a basically New Orleans way of spicing shrimp. An interesting variation (and it will make the dish go further) is to toss in some cooked macaroni shells. The hot spices may be increased or decreased to taste.

Serves 6

1 cup olive oil
Juice of 1 lemon
½ teaspoon paprika
1 bay leaf
1 teaspoon crushed rosemary leaves
¼ teaspoon cayenne pepper
¼ teaspoon crushed oregano
Several dashes Tabasco sauce
Salt and freshly ground pepper to taste
1–2 dashes Worcestershire sauce
30 cloves garlic, parboiled and peeled
1½ pounds shrimp (approximately 20 per pound)
Chopped fresh parsley

1. Gently heat the olive oil in a wide, heavy skillet. Add all the remaining ingredients except the shrimp and parsley. Cook very gently, stirring occasionally, for 15 minutes.

2. Raise the heat and stir in the shrimp. Cook, tossing the shrimp constantly in the hot oil, until they just turn pink and begin to curl. *Do not overcook!*

3. Scrape the shrimp mixture into a bowl. Cover and allow to marinate in the refrigerator for a day or so. Sprinkle with parsley before serving.

FORBIDDEN FLOWER

Over the centuries, nobility has traditionally been horrified by garlic's lingering aroma and earthy pungency. In ancient Rome, laborers and soldiers ate quantities of therapeutic garlic but the senate passed a law forbidding garlic eaters to set foot into the temple of Cybele. Marco Polo, in the thirteenth century, noted that the rich in China preserved their meat in several elegant spices. The poor? They used garlic juice. In the fourteenth century, the King of Castille instituted a law banning knights from his presence for an entire month after they had eaten garlic. In the early 1800s an American cookbook writer stated that garlic, although used gastronomically by the French, was "better adapted to medicine than to cookery." In twentieth-century America, garlic became an accepted ingredient of ethnic, peasant-type cuisines, but a haute cuisine no-no; the posh Four Seasons restaurant in New York, when it first opened, banned garlic in any form.

ASPARAGUS WITH SHRIMP SAUCE

🧄This makes a stunning springtime feast. Everyone hates to hear this, but the asparagus *must* be peeled. Cut off the tough woody portion of each stalk, and peel the asparagus with a swivel-bladed vegetable peeler, from the bottom up to the buds. Then steam it quickly (3 to 7 minutes, depending on size). It will have a heavenly crunch and lack of stringiness, impossible in an un-peeled stalk.

Serves 4

1 pound shrimp
1 2-inch strip of lemon peel
A few peppercorns
1 2-inch stalk of celery with leaves
4 sprigs parsley
11 cloves garlic, 10 peeled and 1 minced
1 tablespoon unsalted butter
½ cup sliced scallions
½ cup vermouth
½ cup whipping cream
Juice of 1 lemon
Salt and freshly ground pepper to taste
2 drops Tabasco sauce

2 pounds asparagus, trimmed, peeled, and steamed until crisp-tender
Chopped fresh parsley

1. Shell and devein shrimp by slitting up the back with a sharp knife and removing the vein. Dice coarsely and reserve.

2. Place the shrimp shells in a saucepan with 2 cups of water, lemon peel, peppercorns, celery, parsley, and the 10 cloves peeled garlic. Bring to a boil, reduce heat, and simmer briskly for 30 minutes. Strain and reserve liquid.

3. Melt the butter in a skillet or sauté pan. Sauté minced garlic and scallions for about 5 minutes, until limp but not brown.

4. Pour in vermouth and ½ cup reserved shrimp stock. Bring to a boil. Add cream and lemon juice. Boil until reduced by half and thickened. Add salt, pepper, and Tabasco.

5. Toss in shrimp and cook briskly, stirring, until the shrimp are *just* cooked. When they turn pink, they are done.

6. Arrange the hot asparagus on a hot platter. Pour the sauce over the asparagus, garnish with parsley, and serve at once.

VENEZUELAN PEPPERS WITH SHRIMP

♣♣ Patrick Burke, chef/owner of Patrick's Café in Atlanta, and his assistant, César Maggio, devised this delicious, extravagant (3 cups of olive oil!), and gloriously messy dish to eat informally with good friends.

Serves 10

3 pounds shrimp (16-20 per pound)
3 cups Spanish olive oil
4 large red bell peppers, seeded and cut into thin julienne strips
8 cloves garlic, peeled and cut into ¼-inch chunks
1 chili pepper, seeded and minced
1 loaf French bread, cut into 1-inch slices
Feta cheese (optional)

"We should be hearing 'please pass the garlic' about as often as we hear 'please pass the salt and pepper.'"

LLOYD J. HARRIS
The Book of Garlic

1. Slit the shrimp up the back with a sharp knife. Remove the vein, but do not peel shrimp. Set them aside.

2. Combine 2 cups of olive oil and the red pepper strips in a deep, heavy skillet or sauté pan. Heat slowly. Cook very gently until the peppers are extremely tender but not at all browned. (The oil will turn a lovely rose color.) Set the peppers aside.

3. Pour the remaining oil into another skillet with the garlic pieces. Stew the garlic slowly for 4 to 5 minutes, until tender and golden. Scoop out the garlic with a strainer or slotted spoon and add it to the peppers.

4. Heat the garlic oil until it ripples. Throw in the minced chili pepper and the shrimp. Sauté, tossing the shrimp in the oil, until they turn pink and are just done.

5. To serve, spoon the peppers and their oil into a serving dish. Surround with shrimp. Serve with bread. Each diner soaks slices of bread in the oil and piles the bread with peppers and garlic. Feta cheese may be eaten with it and the shrimp put on top.

GINGER-GARLIC SHRIMP, CHINA ROYAL

🧄🧄🧄 This is a classic Chinese method of cooking large shrimp, from Frank Ma, an Atlanta restaurateur and enthusiastic home cook. Instruct diners to suck the flavorful garlic-ginger spice coating from the shrimp before shelling. Fresh ginger is available in the produce department of many supermarkets and in all Oriental groceries.

Serves 4

16 jumbo shrimp, with shell
¼ cup vegetable oil
1 piece fresh ginger, 1 inch long, peeled and
    minced
3 cloves garlic, peeled and crushed
2 green onions (scallions), trimmed and
    thinly sliced (green and white parts)
Salt and freshly ground pepper to taste

1. Slit the shrimp up the back with a sharp knife and remove the vein. Do not shell the shrimp.

2. Heat the oil in a wok or wide, heavy skillet. When the oil is rippling, throw in the shrimp and stir-fry over high heat for 2 minutes. Drain very well.

3. Return ½ tablespoon oil to the wok. Heat. Throw in the shrimp along with the ginger, garlic, and onions. Stir-fry for 20 seconds. Season with salt and pepper. Stir-fry for an additional 20 seconds. Serve at once.

SATANIC POWERS

If you loathe garlic because you find it the essence of bad taste and vulgarity, blame Satan for its presence on Earth. According to Mohammed, as Satan strode out of the Garden of Eden after the fall, garlic sprang from his left footstep. (His right? Onion, but that's another story.) But if you love garlic and dote on its assertive perfume, praise Hermes. In Homer's Odyssey, Hermes arms Ulysses with moly—a powerful bulb that many food historians identify as garlic—as protection from Circe and her nasty predilection for turning men into swine. Not only does the bulb protect him from swinehood, but it also causes Circe to fall hopelessly in love with him.

SOLE VERTE WITH DILL SAUCE

🧄🧄 This is an elegant and easy dish for a dinner party from Chef Richard Taylor at Au Provence in Cleveland Heights, Ohio. The green-flecked dill sauce is also good with plain grilled salmon steaks rubbed with a cut clove of garlic or used as a salad dressing.

Serves 10

8 cloves garlic, chopped
1½ cups sliced green onions (scallions)
½ pound carrots, finely diced
1½ sticks unsalted butter
20 shrimp (21–25 per pound)
20 small scallops (about ½ pound)
2 cans (8 ounces each) water chestnuts, drained and sliced
5 pounds sole fillets (8 ounces per person)
5 tablespoons lemon juice
⅔ cup dry white wine
Salt and freshly ground pepper to taste
Dill Sauce (recipe follows)

1. Preheat oven to 400°F.

2. Sauté the garlic, onions, and carrots in 2 tablespoons butter until softened, but do not let them brown. Add the shrimp and scallops and cook briefly. Cool and stir in the water chestnuts.

3. Arrange the sole fillets in a single layer in a buttered baking dish (use 2 dishes if necessary) and top each fillet with 2 tablespoons of the vegetable mixture, 2 shrimp, and 2 scallops. Season the fish with lemon juice, white wine, salt and pepper, and dot with little pieces of the remaining cold butter. Lay a sheet of buttered cooking parchment (cut to the same size as the dish) directly on top of the fish, then cover with aluminum foil.

4. Bake at 400°F. for 10 minutes. Serve with dill sauce.

Dill Sauce

Makes approximately 2 cups

½ cup watercress leaves
¼ cup green onions (scallions), sliced
⅛ cup chopped fresh dill
1 clove garlic, minced
1 cup mayonnaise
2 tablespoons lemon juice
1 tablespoon Cognac
Salt and freshly ground pepper to taste
2 tablespoons good quality oil
½ cup sour cream

1. Combine all the ingredients except the sour cream in a blender jar or food processor. Mix until creamy.

2. Remove the sauce from the blender. Taste for seasoning, adjust if needed, add sour cream, and mix well.

3. Chill before serving.

GROUPER FILLETS IN GARLIC-VERMOUTH SAUCE

It is important here, as in any fish dish, not to overcook, or the fish will be dry and unpalatable. The garlic-vermouth sauce is silken and delicate.

Serves 6

6 grouper fillets, 6 ounces each
Salt and freshly ground pepper to taste
30 cloves garlic, parboiled, peeled, and sim-
    mered in water or stock for 20 minutes
½ cup dry vermouth
4 tablespoons softened unsalted butter, cut in
    pieces

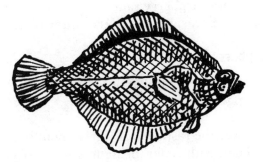

1. Preheat oven to 400°F.

2. Make ready a piece of buttered cooking parchment.

3. Place the grouper fillets in one layer in a shallow baking dish. Sprinkle with salt and pepper. Scatter the prepared garlic cloves around and over the fish. Pour vermouth around the fish. Cover the fillets with the buttered parchment.

4. Place the baking dish in the preheated oven for 10 minutes, until the fish fillets are opaque and just done.

5. Remove and discard the paper. Remove the fillets to a serving platter and keep warm. Pour the juices and garlic into a small saucepan.

6. Bring the juices to a boil, stirring vigorously with a wooden spoon to partially mash the garlic cloves. Boil until syrupy and reduced by a little more than half. With a fork, swirl in the pieces of butter.

7. Pour the sauce over the fish and serve at once.

BRAISED STURGEON WITH GARLIC-RASPBERRY SAUCE

🧄🧄Raspberries and garlic, as this recipe from Jimella Lucas of The Ark restaurant in Nahcotta, Washington, proves, are wonderful together. This dish was featured during The Ark's Garlic Festival. If sturgeon is unavailable in your area, substitute grouper fillets.

Serves 4

5 tablespoons clarified butter
4 6-ounce fillets of fresh sturgeon
Salt and white pepper to taste
Juice from ½ lemon
¼ cup plus 2 tablespoons Madeira
1 teaspoon minced garlic
½ teaspoon chopped shallots
Raspberry Purée (recipe follows)
2 tablespoons heavy cream
Few fresh rasperries for garnish

1. Preheat oven to 300°F.

2. Melt the butter in a sauté pan.

3. Place the fillets in the pan, season lightly with salt and white pepper. Brown the fillets on both sides over medium-high heat and sauté until fillets are about half-cooked. Squeeze lemon juice over the fillets.

4. Deglaze pan with ¼ cup of the Madeira. Remove the pan from the heat. Transfer the fillets to an ovenproof plate and keep them warm in the oven. The fillets will finish cooking while the sauce is being made.

5. Put the sauté pan back on the heat, add the minced garlic and shallots, shake the pan to agitate the contents until the garlic becomes light golden.

6. Add the remaining 2 tablespoons Madeira, stir lightly to deglaze pan and mix thoroughly. Add the raspberry purée and cook gently for 2 to 3 minutes to slightly reduce the mixture and marry the flavors. Stir in the heavy cream; heat just until the sauce is warmed and blended.

7. Remove the fillets from the oven. Top the fillets with raspberry sauce and garnish with 3 or 4 fresh raspberries. Serve immediately.

Raspberry Purée

10 ounces fresh raspberries (about 2 cups)
¼ cup water

Pick over the raspberries. Place them in a saucepan with water, bring to simmer over medium-low heat, and cook to a soft purée, stirring occasionally. Sieve through a fine-meshed strainer to remove seeds.

Chicken

"There are many good dishes in which twenty cloves to a pound or so of garlic appear without overwhelming either the house or its inhabitants.... But one unusual consequence is always noticed by those not accustomed to garlic in quantity; there is a feeling of complete clearness of the respiratory organs! An amazing sensation of liberation in the head, and it is as if one had acquired a completely new sense of smell."

SYLVIA WINDLE HUMPHREY
A Matter of Taste, 1965

WHOLE GARLIC BAKED IN A CHICKEN

🧄 Another variation on the theme of roasted garlic. The beauty of this dish is in its simplicity, but you might want to add fresh herbs and roast some small potatoes along with the bird.

Serves 6

3 heads garlic
1 5- to 6-pound roasting chicken
Salt and freshly ground pepper
1 lemon
Olive oil
2 onions
¼ cup chicken stock
¼ cup sherry, dry vermouth, or white wine

THE STRENGTH OF GARLIC

Garlic buffs like to believe that garlic was used to strengthen and sustain the pyramid builders in ancient times. One persistent rumor, started by the Greek historian Herodotus in 450 B.C., deals with the Cheops Pyramid, built in 2900 B.C., and the staggering sum of 1,600 talents of silver (the equivalent of about two million dollars) spent on radishes, onions, and garlic to feed the builders.

---

1. Preheat oven to 375°F.

2. Prepare 3 whole heads of garlic, as for Roasted Garlic (see page 14).

3. Season a 5- to 6-pound roasting chicken with salt and freshly ground pepper. Rub inside and out with lemon and a little olive oil. Place the 3 heads of garlic in the cavity of the bird. Fold the wings back but do not truss the bird—the heat will penetrate to the thighs more efficiently if left untrussed.

4. Slice a couple of onions into a roasting pan and add the chicken stock and the sherry, dry vermouth, or white wine. Place the chicken on a rack in the pan and roast in the preheated oven for about 1½ hours until done, but not overdone. (The juices will run *almost* clear, with just the faintest tinge of pink.) Start roasting breast-down, then turn on one side, next the other, and finish breast-up. Baste occasionally, adding extra stock and wine as needed.

5. To serve, carve the chicken (let it stand for 10 minutes first so the juices can settle) and present it on a platter with the heads of garlic. Degrease the pan juices and pass them in a pitcher.

YOGURT CHICKEN WITH GARLIC-MINT DIPPING SAUCE

🧄Chicken "oven-fried" in this manner becomes extremely juicy. Do not pour the sauce over the chicken. Each bit of chicken is dipped into the sauce and then eaten. The dipping sauce is also delicious with fried shrimp.

Serves 4

1½ cups plain yogurt
1 cup bread crumbs
Salt and freshly ground pepper to taste
4 chicken thighs, skinned
4 chicken legs, skinned
Dipping Sauce (recipe follows)

1. Preheat oven to 400°F.

2. Pour the yogurt into a wide, shallow bowl and set it on your work surface.

3. Season the bread crumbs with salt and pepper. Spread crumbs out on a platter and place next to the yogurt.

4. Place a wire rack over a baking sheet and set it aside.

5. Dry the chicken pieces. Dip each piece into the yogurt until thoroughly coated on both sides. Then roll each piece in the crumbs, pressing the piece in so that the crumbs ad-

here. Each piece should be evenly coated.

6. Place the chicken on the wire rack. Bake for 40 to 45 minutes.

7. To serve, place a piece of chicken on each of 4 small plates. Pour some sauce in a crescent on the bottom edge of each plate, around the chicken but not on it. Place the remaining chicken on a platter and pass the remaining sauce in a clear pitcher. Serve hot or at room temperature.

Dipping Sauce

1 cup plain yogurt
Garlic purée from 1 head of Roasted Garlic (see pages 14-15)
½ small onion, coarsely chopped
1 thin slice ginger root, peeled and chopped
2 tablespoons chopped green chilies (canned), drained
1 teaspoon sugar
Salt to taste
¾ cup fresh mint leaves
¼ cup fresh coriander (Chinese parsley) leaves
¼ cup fresh parsley leaves

Place all the ingredients in a blender or food processor. Flick the motor on and off until a thin, flecked green sauce is achieved. Serve at once.

CHICKEN AND SAUSAGE IN TOMATO SAUCE

🧄🧄 This is an ethnic family favorite, from an ebullient sausage maker, Paul Masselli, of Lilburn, Georgia. This dish may be made several days in advance and reheated.

Serves 8

¼ cup olive oil
4 large cloves garlic, coarsely chopped
2 ½ pounds sweet Italian sausage links
1 ½ pounds hot Italian sausage links
4 chicken legs
4 chicken thighs
2 cans (1 pound 12 ounces each) tomatoes
1 can (6 ounces) tomato paste
Salt and freshly ground pepper to taste
½ tablespoon dried basil
½ cup dry red wine
Chopped fresh parsley

1. Heat the oil in a large, heavy skillet. Add the garlic and sauté until light golden. Remove the garlic and reserve.

2. Prick the sausages in several places and then sear them in the hot oil. Remove and set aside, covered.

3. Brown chicken well on all sides in the same skillet. Remove and set aside, covered.

4. Pour 1 tablespoon of the drippings into a large Dutch oven or casserole. Discard the remaining drippings or save them for another use. (Do not wash skillet; you will need it later.) Crush the tomatoes with your hands and add them, with their juice, to the drippings. Add the tomato paste, salt, pepper, basil, and reserved garlic. Simmer, uncovered, for 15 minutes.

5. Add the sausage and simmer, covered, for 20 minutes.

6. Add the chicken, cover, and simmer for 20 minutes more.

7. Meanwhile, deglaze the skillet with the wine. Stir the wine into the sauce and simmer for a final 10 minutes. Sprinkle with parsley. Serve with pasta and freshly grated Parmesan cheese.

CONSUELO'S CHICKEN ADOBO

🧄🧄 Magellan found the Philippines while searching for spice routes. He also found that garlic was an important foodstuff on those islands. Filippino food has evolved into a fascinating blend of Oriental and Spanish flavors and techniques, and garlic is still as important as ever. Chicken *adobo* is considered the Philippine national dish. This dish may be made a day or two in advance. Just scrape off any congealed fat and discard, then reheat gently.

Serves 6

½ cup soy sauce
6 tablespoons wine vinegar
9 cloves garlic, 5 peeled and crushed, 4 minced
6 bay leaves
2 tablespoons sugar
15 peppercorns
6 chicken legs
6 chicken thighs
Water
1 teaspoon sesame oil
3 large onions, sliced thin

1. Combine the soy sauce, vinegar, 5 crushed garlic cloves, bay leaves, sugar, and peppercorns. Arrange the chicken in a wide, shallow pottery or glass bowl. Pour the vinegar-soy mixture over the chicken. Add water so the marinade almost covers it. Turn the chicken pieces to coat them with the marinade and let them marinate for several hours at room temperature or 24 hours in the refrigerator. Turn the chicken a few times during this period.

2. Brush a wide, heavy skillet with sesame oil. Heat.

3. Drain the chicken and dry the pieces on paper towels. Reserve the marinade. Fry the chicken, skin-side down, in the hot skillet. The chicken will render its own fat. Turn and fry until richly browned on both sides, but not cooked through. Remove the chicken from the skillet.

4. To the fat in the skillet, add the onions and garlic. Cook slowly, scraping browned particles from the skillet with a wooden spoon, until the onions turn amber. Do not let the garlic burn.

5. Return the chicken to the skillet. Strain the marinade over the chicken. Bring to a simmer, cover, and simmer until chicken is cooked through, 25 minutes or so. Remove the chicken, cover it, and keep it warm.

6. Degrease the pan juices as thoroughly as possible. Boil the pan juices in the skillet until reduced somewhat and thickened. Recombine the chicken and the sauce. Traditionally, this should be served warm or at room temperature, not steaming hot.

CHICKEN WITH AVOCADO IN GARLIC CREAM

🧄This dish is a sensual experience—in fact, it is downright sexy. It is important to cook the chicken until it is *just* done, so that the texture is creamy. If it cooks longer, it becomes tough and stringy.

Serves 6–8

10 cloves garlic, peeled
3 cups whipping cream
Juice of 2 limes plus some extra
Dash or two of Tabasco
Salt and freshly ground white pepper to taste
2 ripe avocados
4 chicken breasts, split, skinned, and boned
Pinch cinnamon
½ teaspoon dried tarragon
4 tablespoons unsalted butter

1. Preheat oven to 325°F.

2. Combine the garlic and cream in a deep, heavy saucepan. Simmer until the garlic is very tender and the cream is thickened and reduced by about half. Stir frequently and do not allow it to scorch or boil over.

3. Rub the garlic and cream through a sieve. Return to saucepan. Stir the juice of 2 limes and the Tabasco into the sauce. Season with salt and pepper. Set aside with a piece of plastic wrap directly over the surface of the sauce, to prevent a skin forming.

4. Halve the avocados, remove the pits and skin, and cut into ½-inch-thick slices. Toss with lime juice to prevent darkening, cover with plastic wrap, and set aside.

5. Remove the small "fillet" from beneath each chicken breast half. Save for another use (stir-fries or chicken salad, for instance). Trim all fat, skin, gristle, and connective tissue from the chicken breast halves. Sprinkle each with salt, pepper, cinnamon, and tarragon.

6. Heat the butter in a wide, heavy skillet. Place the chicken in the skillet and sauté gently for 1 minute on each side. The breasts must not touch each other in the pan and they must not brown. They will just begin to turn white. (Do the sautéing in two batches.)

7. Place the sautéed breast halves on an attractive ovenproof platter and place it in the oven for 7 to 10 minutes, or until just done. The breasts are done when they feel firm and springy, not soft and mushy. If you are not sure, cut into one—it should be opaque with just the faintest blush of pink.

8. While the chicken is in the oven, warm the garlic cream sauce. Turn the avocado slices

54

in the hot butter left in the chicken skillet, just to warm them slightly.

9. When the chicken is done, place some avocado slices on each breast. Mask with the hot garlic cream sauce. Serve at once.

"The smell of this plant is generally considered offensive and it is the most acrimonious in its taste."
MRS. BEETON
Cookery and Household Management, 1836

CHICKEN BRAISED WITH 40 CLOVES OF GARLIC

This is my version of the classic that started so many (including me) on the road to garlic passion. Forty cloves are traditional, but more wouldn't hurt. If you are in a hurry, don't bother to parboil and peel the garlic. Simply add them unpeeled and let the diners mash down on the soft, cooked cloves with their forks. The buttery garlic will pop out.

Serves 6

40 cloves garlic, parboiled and peeled
6 chicken legs/thighs (chicken may be
    skinned, if desired)
2 onions, coarsely chopped
2 tablespoons olive oil
1 cup chopped fresh parsley
1 teaspoon dried tarragon, crumbled
½ teaspoon allspice
¼ teaspoon cinnamon
Salt and freshly ground pepper to taste
¼ cup Cognac
⅓ cup dry white vermouth

1. Preheat oven to 375°F.

2. Place all the ingredients in a deep, heavy pot that can be covered. Combine everything very well with your hands. Seal the pot very tightly with foil. Place a cover over the foil. The pot must be very well sealed so that no juices or steam can escape.

3. Bake for 1½ hours. Do not open the pot during this time.

4. Serve piping hot, with good crusty bread for mopping up the juices and garlic. Open the pot at the table, so that the diners may get the full benefit of the marvelous fragrance that explodes out of the vessel.

ROAST CHICKEN IN SHERRY VINEGAR AND GARLIC SAUCE

🧄🧄 Cookbook author and teacher Perla Meyers loves garlic and uses it in many ways, both traditional and innovative. Here, chickens are roasted with whole cloves and sherry vinegar. The final sauce, enriched by *crème fraîche,* is rich, highly flavorful, and dazzling. The *crème fraîche* needs to be made ahead, as it can take from 8 to 24 hours to sour and thicken, depending mainly on the temperature of your kitchen. It will keep in the refrigerator for 10 days to 2 weeks, but it cannot be frozen.

Serves 8

2 roasting chickens (about 2¾ pounds each)
Salt and freshly ground pepper to taste
Paprika
Thyme
Dijon mustard
18 large cloves garlic, 2 crushed and 16 peeled
2 tablespoons unsalted butter
A little olive oil
½ cup sherry vinegar
1 cup chicken stock
1 cup *Crème Fraîche* (recipe follows)
2 teaspoons tomato paste
2 teaspoons Dijon mustard
1 tablespoon Cognac
Beurre Manié (recipe follows)

For Garnish
2 tomatoes, diced
Fresh parsley and chives, finely minced

1. Preheat oven to 375°F.

2. Season the chickens with salt, pepper, paprika, thyme, Dijon mustard, and crushed garlic. Truss the chickens.

3. In a large, heavy, ovenproof baking dish, heat the butter and olive oil. Brown the chickens lightly on both sides and remove them to a platter. Deglaze the baking dish with the sherry vinegar. Add the 16 peeled cloves of garlic to the dish and return the chickens. Place the dish in the oven. Add a little sherry vinegar to the dish every 10 minutes as you baste the chicken.

4. Continue roasting and basting the chicken with chicken stock, taking care not to burn the garlic cloves. When done (1 to 1½ hours), remove the chickens to a roasting pan and put them under the broiler to brown evenly. Carve the chickens and keep them warm.

5. Pass the pan juices through a fine sieve, pressing down on the garlic cloves to extract all of their pulp. Thoroughly degrease the pan juices and set the pan over direct heat.

6. Add the *crème fraîche,* which has been mixed together with the tomato paste, Dijon mustard, and Cognac, and cook the sauce until it thickens. If necessary, whisk in a little *beurre manié* as it cooks to ensure thickening.

7. Add the diced fresh tomatoes and spoon a little of the sauce onto each serving plate. Top with some carved chicken and sprinkle with parsley and chives. Serve at once.

Crème Fraîche

Makes about 2 cups

2 cups heavy whipping cream (nonultra pasteurized)
3 tablespoons buttermilk

1. Combine the cream and buttermilk in a glass jar and whisk until well blended. Cover the jar and set it aside in a warm, draft-free place until the cream sours and thickens.

2. Stir thoroughly, cover and chill, then use in recipes as indicated.

Beurre Manié

1 tablespoon flour
1 tablespoon softened unsalted butter

Knead together until a smooth paste is formed.

NUTRITION

Garlic as an accent in traditional cookery was used in such negligible quantities that its daily nutritional contribution was minimal. When used as a vegetable or major ingredient in a recipe, however, it becomes worthy of noting.

Two large heads of garlic weigh about 100 grams. This much garlic contributes 137 calories, which is divided primarily between carbohydrates and protein. The 6.2 grams of protein contained in the garlic provides about 10 percent of the adult U.S. RDA (required daily amount) of protein. Garlic also has significant amounts of vitamin C. A whopping 25 percent of the U.S. RDA is contributed by 100 grams of garlic. Thiamine, an important B vitamin, is also plentiful in garlic. Two heads supply about 17 percent of the U.S. RDA of this essential nutrient. Other significant nutrients are riboflavin, 5.3 percent; calcium, 3 percent; niacin, 2.5 percent; and phosphorus, 20 percent of the U.S. RDA. Garlic contributes very little sodium or fat and no cholesterol.

If you needed a nutritional justification for pleasing your palate, garlic certainly passes muster.

"Garlic can make any cook famous."
LORIS TROUP
The Tasting Spoon, 1955

ANNE DISRUDE'S CHICKEN WITH RASPBERRIES

🧄 Another pairing of garlic with raspberries. This dish—quite different from The Ark's Sturgeon in Raspberry-Garlic Sauce—appeared in *Food and Wine* magazine.

Serves 2

16 medium garlic cloves, peeled
1 tablespoon sugar
¼ cup plus 1 teaspoon raspberry vinegar
½ cup water
2 chicken breast halves, boned, with skin attached (about 12 ounces)
2 tablespoons plus 1 teaspoon unsalted butter, cold
1 teaspoon vegetable oil
¼ teaspoon salt
¼ teaspoon freshly ground pepper
¼ cup fresh raspberries

1. In a small saucepan, combine the garlic cloves, sugar, 1 teaspoon of the vinegar, and ½ cup water. Bring to a boil over high heat. Reduce the heat to low and simmer, uncovered, until the sugar dissolves, about 3 minutes. Increase the heat to moderate, cover, and cook until the garlic is tender enough to pierce with a fork, about 10 minutes.

2. Uncover the saucepan, increase the heat to high, and cook until the liquid is reduced to a thick syrup and the garlic is caramelized, about 10 minutes.

3. Add the remaining ¼ cup of vinegar and cook for 30 seconds to dissolve any sugar clinging to the pan. Set the sauce aside.

4. Cut each chicken breast half crosswise into 5 slices; leave the skin on. Pat dry.

5. In a large, heavy, nonreactive (see page 10) skillet, melt 1 teaspoon of the butter in the oil over high heat until sizzling. Add the chicken pieces, skin-side down. Reduce the heat to moderate and sauté until the skin is well browned, about 3 minutes. Turn and cook until browned on the second side, about 3 minutes. Remove the chicken to a plate and cover loosely to keep warm. Pour off any fat in the pan.

6. Add the reserved sauce with garlic cloves to the skillet. Bring to a boil over high heat, scraping up any browned bits from the bottom of the pan. Continue to boil for 1 to 2 minutes, until the sauce is thick and syrupy. Remove from the heat. Season with the salt and pepper. Whisk in the remaining 2 tablespoons of cold butter, 1 tablespoon at a time.

7. Return the chicken with any accumulated juices to the skillet. Toss gently to coat with the sauce. Add the raspberries and toss gently again. Serve hot.

Meat

"Garlic is of course essential to my private cooking."

M.F.K. FISHER

With Bold Knife and Fork, 1969

MEAT LOAF

🧄🧄There is something comforting about a meat loaf. This one is full of herbs, garlic, and pine nuts. Serve it hot, or cold on crusty bread, with Onion-Garlic Relish, (see page 29) if desired.

Serves 6 with leftovers for sandwiches

3 large cloves garlic
½ cup fresh parsley
½ cup fresh basil
1 pound ground beef chuck
1 pound ground veal
1 pound ground pork shoulder
2 extra-large eggs
½ cup bread crumbs
½ cup grated Romano cheese
1 ½ ounces pine nuts
Salt and freshly ground pepper to taste
¼ cup tomato purée
Bacon strips

1. Preheat oven to 325° F.

2. Chop together the garlic, parsley, and basil.

3. Combine all the ingredients, except the bacon, in a large bowl. Mix them together thoroughly with the hands. Fry a tiny portion and taste for seasoning. Add more salt and pepper if necessary.

4. Place some bacon strips on the bottom of a round, shallow baking dish. Form the meat mixture into a fat, round, compact loaf, pressing it together tightly. Place the loaf on the bacon strips and cover the top with additional strips of bacon.

5. Bake uncovered in the preheated oven for 1 ½ hours or until an instant-read thermometer registers 170° F. Drain the fat from the baking pan twice during the baking time. When done, allow the loaf to stand for 15 minutes before slicing and serving.

VEAL ESTERHAZY

❦ Ron Cohn is an imaginative and talented chef who once ran an Atlanta restaurant called Hal's. Veal Esterházy is Ron's adaptation of a traditional Hungarian beef dish.

Serves 6

¼ pound plus 2 tablespoons unsalted butter
8 cloves garlic, parboiled and peeled
1 large onion, chopped
2 carrots, peeled and chopped
2 stalks celery, chopped
2 small parsnips, peeled and chopped
2 cups stock or water
1 bay leaf
Salt and freshly ground pepper to taste
Grated rind of 1 lemon
Juice of ½ lemon
1 tablespoon Dijon mustard
1 tablespoon flour whisked into 3 tablespoons
    water
1 cup sour cream, at room temperature
12 small veal scaloppine
Flour
2 tablespoons corn oil
Chopped fresh parsley

1. Heat ¼ pound butter in a heavy saucepan. Sauté the garlic and vegetables gently until almost tender but not browned.

2. Add the stock or water, bay leaf, salt, pepper, lemon rind, and lemon juice. Let simmer gently until the vegetables are very tender. Discard the bay leaf. Put the mixture into the jar of a blender or food processor and purée, or push through a sieve. Return the purée to the saucepan.

3. Stir the mustard, flour-water, and sour cream into the purée. Bring to a simmer and cook gently for about 5 minutes. Taste and adjust seasonings. Keep warm.

4. Place the scaloppine on a sheet of waxed paper and cover with another sheet. With a meat mallet, pound gently until the cutlets are about ⅛ inch thick and of even thickness.

5. Spread flour on a sheet of clean waxed paper and season with salt and pepper.

6. Heat the remaining 2 tablespoons butter and the oil in a large skillet. Dry the veal, dredge in seasoned flour, shake off the excess. When the butter-oil mixture is hot but not brown, cook the veal quickly—about 1½ minutes on each side over moderately high heat. They should be browned and just barely cooked through. Do them in batches, wiping out the pan and adding more oil and butter as necessary. They must not be crowded in the pan. As they are done, remove to a platter and keep warm.

7. Spoon some of the hot sauce onto each of 6 hot plates. Place 2 veal scaloppine on each. Garnish with parsley and serve at once. Serve the rest of the sauce at the table.

VEAL DUMPLINGS WITH STEAMED RED PEPPER STRIPS

🧄🧄You could call these meatballs, of course, but it sounds so dull. The little parsley-and-garlic-flecked morsels of tender veal, surrounded by meaty sweet pepper strips, are much too elegant for such a pedestrian name.

Serves 6–8

2 pounds ground veal
1 cup bread crumbs or matzoh meal
4 large eggs
4 tablespoons chopped fresh parsley
6 cloves garlic, finely chopped
Salt and freshly ground pepper to taste
Grated rind of 2 lemons
Juice of 2 lemons
6 tablespoons freshly grated Parmesan cheese
Corn oil
3 cups chicken stock
Steamed Red Pepper strips (recipe follows)
Chopped parsley

1. Combine veal, bread crumbs or matzoh meal, eggs, parsley, garlic, salt and pepper, lemon rind and juice, and Parmesan cheese in a large bowl. Use your hands to combine well. Fry a tiny piece in a small skillet and taste. Adjust seasonings to your liking.

2. Form the mixture into small balls (about the size of walnuts). Film a large heavy skillet with corn oil to a depth of ⅛ inch. Heat. Sauté the meatballs (do them in batches and don't crowd them) in the skillet until they are browned and crusty on the outside and just cooked through (5 to 7 minutes for each batch). Replace oil as needed.

3. As they are done, transfer the dumplings to a paper-towel-lined plate and blot well. When all are cooked and blotted, spread them out in a wide, shallow dish, cover with plastic wrap, and refrigerate until needed. They will keep for 3 to 4 days.

4. To heat and serve, pour the chicken stock into a pot. Bring to a boil. Add the veal dumplings and simmer gently for 5 to 10 minutes until heated through. Remove the dumplings with a slotted spoon, and arrange them in the center of an attractive platter. Surround with the steamed red pepper strips, sprinkle with chopped parsley, and serve at once.

Steamed Red Peppers

6 red bell peppers
1½ tablespoons olive oil
1½ tablespoons unsalted butter

1. Remove the stems from the peppers and

cut each in half. Remove the seeds and ribs. Cut the peppers lengthwise into strips about 1 inch wide.

2. Heat the oil and butter in a wide skillet.

3. Toss in the peppers and stir-fry them over moderately high heat for 1 minute. Do not let them brown.

4. Turn off the heat, clap a tight-fitting lid on the skillet, and let the peppers steam for 5 to 7 minutes. The peppers will be meaty and tender with a hint of remaining crispness. They may wait, uncovered, for an hour or so. Reheat briefly before serving. Arrange the peppers on the platter surrounding the veal dumplings, and pour the pan juices over.

OTHER USES FOR VEAL DUMPLINGS

Use the mixture to stuff cabbage leaves. One pound of veal will stuff the leaves from 1 medium cabbage. Simmer the stuffed leaves in chicken stock, flavored with fresh lemon juice, or a light tomato sauce flavored with lemon rind.

Serve veal dumplings with linguine and fresh tomato sauce.

Simmer raw dumplings in rich, well-seasoned chicken stock until just done. Stir in a handful of trimmed raw spinach leaves at the last minute. Pass a bowl of grated Parmesan cheese at the table.

Use the uncooked dumpling mixture to stuff a veal breast.

KOREAN BUL GOGI

🧄🧄*Bul Gogi* is splendid when grilled over charcoal, but oven broiling will do nicely if charcoal is not possible.

Serves 6–8

1½ tablespoons chopped fresh ginger
20 cloves garlic, peeled and crushed
2 bunches scallions, sliced—green and white parts
1 cup sugar
1 cup soy sauce
¼ cup sesame oil
2 cups water
2 flank steaks

1. In a bowl, combine all the ingredients except the flank steaks.

2. Place the steaks in one layer in a nonreactive (see page 10) baking dish. Pour in the marinade. Allow to marinate, at room temperature, for 6 hours, or in the refrigerator for 12 or more. Turn occasionally.

3. Remove the steaks from the marinade. Grill or broil to a state of juicy rareness. Let stand for 5 minutes. Slice thinly against the grain, and serve at once, with rice. (The marinade may be used again. Boil for a few minutes, then refrigerate until needed.)

VEAL SHANKS WITH WILD MUSHROOMS

🧄Dried cèpes and morels can be purchased in many specialty food stores or the gourmet department of some supermarkets, but feel free to substitute if necessary. I have successfully made it with a mixture of fresh cultivated mushrooms and dried Chinese mushrooms or Japanese shitake mushrooms, available from Oriental food stores.

Serves 6

1 ounce dried cèpes
1 ounce dried morels
Flour
Salt and freshly ground pepper to taste
6 tablespoons unsalted butter
3 tablespoons vegetable oil
6 slices veal shank, each about 1½ inches
   thick
1 cup dry white wine
20 cloves garlic, unpeeled
Veal or beef stock

1. Soak the dried mushrooms in warm water, to cover generously, for 2 hours. Strain the water through a cheesecloth-lined sieve or a coffee filter and reserve. Rinse the mushrooms under cold running tap water, and trim off and discard any tough stems.

2. Spread flour on a sheet of waxed paper. Season with salt and pepper.

3. Heat 3 tablespoons of the butter and the oil in a wide, deep, heavy, nonreactive (see page 10) skillet. Dredge the veal shanks in the seasoned flour. Sauté over medium heat until well browned on both sides. Transfer to a platter.

4. Pour the fat out of the skillet. Add the white wine and 1 cup of the mushroom-soaking liquid. Bring to a boil and let boil for 2 minutes, scraping the bottom of the pan with a wooden spoon or spatula. Reduce heat.

5. Return the veal shanks to the skillet. Scatter in the garlic cloves. Season with salt and pepper to taste. Let simmer, covered, for about 20 minutes.

6. Meanwhile, heat the remaining 3 tablespoons butter in a skillet. Sauté the mushrooms in the butter, stirring occasionally, for 5 minutes.

7. When the veal shanks have cooked for 20 minutes, turn them over. Add enough stock to barely cover the veal shanks and add the sautéed mushrooms to the skillet. Cover and let the meat simmer for another 1½ hours or until it is meltingly tender and falling off the bones, and the liquid has cooked down to a thick, rich sauce. Baste with the pan juices occasionally.

8. Remove the veal and mushrooms to a serving platter, cover tightly, and keep warm. Sieve the pan liquid, pressing down on the garlic so that the pulp rubs through. Skim the fat from the sauce. Reheat briefly, then pour over the veal.

9. Serve at once with small spoons or forks for digging the delicious marrow out of the bones.

PORT-GLAZED RIBS

Both the meaty ribs and the garlic cloves caramelize as they cook in the white port. This is a dish to be eaten with the hands. Gnawing at the bones provides much pleasure.

Serves 2–4

⅓ cup vegetable oil
8 meaty country-style pork ribs
1–1¼ cups white port (California will do, but the real thing, from Portugal, is best)
Salt and freshly ground pepper to taste
40 cloves garlic, unpeeled
½ cup chicken stock

1. Heat the oil in a wide, heavy skillet. Add the ribs in one layer, and brown them well, turning with tongs as they cook to brown on all sides. When this is done, remove the ribs to a platter.

2. Pour out the fat. Pour the port into the skillet and bring to a boil. (Avert your face; the port may flame.) Stir and scrape the bottom of the skillet to loosen the browned bits. Return the ribs to the skillet. Season with salt and pepper. Scatter in the garlic cloves.

3. Reduce the heat, cover the skillet, and let the ribs cook in the port. From time to time, uncover to turn the ribs and stir up the garlic. After about 25 minutes, if the ribs have released a quantity of liquid, pour it off. Add ¼ cup port to skillet and proceed. Cook for about 45 to 55 minutes or until the ribs are tender but not dried out and the garlic is tender. At the end of the cooking time, the ribs will be very dark brown and glazed—almost candied—and the liquid will have cooked down to almost nothing. If, at any time during the cooking, things threaten to burn, add just a bit of port.

4. Remove the ribs and garlic to a serving platter and keep warm. Pour the stock into the skillet and bring to a boil. Boil, stirring and scraping, for a few minutes, until a thick dark sauce is formed.

5. Pour over the ribs and serve at once.

HUNGARIAN BEEF STEW WITH MUSHROOMS

♣ Second-cut brisket (sometimes called deckle) makes succulent beef stew meat. My second choice is beef shoulder. In this stew, the traditional Hungarian flavors of paprika, marjoram, and dill are heightened with the subtle accent of roasted garlic purée, swirled in at the last minute.

Serves 6

3 tablespoons unsalted butter
3 large onions, coarsely chopped
2 tablespoons Hungarian paprika
2 pounds mushrooms, quartered
3 pounds well-trimmed beef stew meat, cut into 1-inch cubes
Salt and freshly ground pepper to taste
1 teaspoon marjoram
3 tablespoons tomato paste
1 cup sour cream, at room temperature
1 tablespoon flour
3 tablespoons chopped fresh dill or 1 teaspoon dried
Purée from 1 to 2 heads Roasted Garlic (see pages 14-15)

1. Preheat oven to 300° F.

2. Melt the butter in a heavy pot that can be covered. Sauté the onions until tender.

3. Add the paprika, and stir over very low heat until the onions are coated with the paprika.

4. Add the mushrooms and stir. Cook over low heat for a few minutes.

5. Toss in the beef cubes, remaining seasonings, and tomato paste. Cover the pot tightly and bake for 1½ hours or more until the meat is very tender. Lower the oven temperature during this time so that the contents of the pot remain at a gentle simmer. The stew may be prepared to this point, covered and refrigerated. Next day, scrape off any congealed fat, bring to a simmer, and proceed.

6. With a whisk, beat the sour cream, flour, and dill together. Swirl in the garlic purée. Stir the mixture into the stew.

7. Bring to a simmer and cook over very low heat for 10 minutes, stirring occasionally. Serve at once.

GARLIC CARBONNADE OF BEEF

When stewing beef, the liquid will cook away if the pot is too deep. Choose a heavy pot deep enough to accommodate the ingredients and the juices that will form, but not too deep. An enameled cast-iron paella pot (it can be covered tightly with foil) or an enameled cast-iron deep skillet with a cover (called a chicken fryer) are excellent for this dish and the next one.

Serves 6

¼ pound bacon, coarsely diced
4 large onions, cut in half and sliced into thin half moons
30 cloves garlic, parboiled and peeled
1 tablespoon brown sugar
½ teaspoon thyme
1 bay leaf
Salt and freshly ground pepper to taste
12 ounces (1½ cups) dark beer
2 tablespoons wine vinegar
3 pounds well-trimmed beef stew meat, cut into 1-inch cubes

1. Sauté the bacon in a shallow, heavy pot until crisp. Remove with a slotted spoon and reserve.

2. Stir the onions and garlic into the hot fat in the pot. Cover and cook over very low heat for 15 minutes.

3. Uncover, sprinkle the vegetables with sugar, and cook over moderately high heat, stirring frequently, until they are very dark brown.

4. Stir in the seasonings, ¾ cup of the beer, and the wine vinegar. Boil while stirring and scraping the bottom of the pot. Add the beef and the remaining beer. Bring to a simmer, cover tightly, and simmer gently for 1½ hours or until the meat is very tender.

5. Remove the meat from the pot to a bowl and cover tightly so that the beef does not dry out. Skim the fat from the sauce. Strain the pot liquid through a sieve, rubbing the garlic and onion through so that they purée. Return the sauce to the pot. If it is thin, boil it rapidly until it is thick, enough to coat a spoon. Taste and add salt, pepper, or a bit more vinegar to taste. Recombine the beef and sauce, add the reserved bacon, heat, and serve at once.

STEFADO OF BEEF AND GARLIC

🧄This is a wonderful, peasant beef stew. The garnish of feta cheese and walnuts gives it an intriguing texture and temperature contrast. Notice that my recipes for stew call for no preliminary browning of the meat. The meat will be, nevertheless, richly flavored and tender. This can be made in advance and refrigerated for several days. The flavor improves with each reheating.

Serves 6

GARLIC MEDICINE

Modern health-food stores have shelves of garlic capsules recommended for a variety of ills, and medical researchers (particularly in Europe and the Orient) publish papers every now and then reporting on the possible medicinal effects of garlic. "Garlic is Italian Drano," said an Italian pizza maker to me. "It clears out the blood." Indeed, there are experiments in the medical literature implicating garlic as an agent in cholesterol control. Other researchers are working with garlic's antibacterial, antifungal, and possible anticarcinogenic properties and are investigating its use in controlling blood pressure.

3 pounds well-trimmed stewing beef, cut into 1-inch cubes
1 6-ounce can of tomato paste
½ cup chopped fresh parsley
Salt and freshly ground pepper to taste
1 bay leaf
1 teaspoon dried oregano, crumbled
1 teaspoon cinnamon
1 teaspoon ground cumin
½ teaspoon sugar
½ cup dry white wine
¼ cup red wine vinegar
1 pound small pearl onions, parboiled and peeled
30 cloves garlic, parboiled and peeled
½ pound feta cheese, crumbled
1 cup walnuts, coarsely chopped
½ cup chopped fresh parsley

1. Preheat oven to 350° F.

2. In a heavy pot that can be covered, combine all the ingredients except the feta, walnuts, and ½ cup of the parsley.

3. Cover tightly and bake for 1 ½ hours or more, until the meat is very tender. Lower the oven temperature during this time, so that the contents of the pot remain at a gentle simmer.

4. Skim off the fat. Do not boil the sauce down; it should remain rather thin. Ladle the stew into a deep platter. Garnish with feta, walnuts, and the remaining parsley.

COWBOY'S BRISKET

♧ ♧ There is no cut of beef more suited to pot roasting than brisket. This particular brisket is adapted from the old Southwest chuckwagon custom of braising a tough cut of beef with coffee. The coffee gravy is full-bodied and mouth-watering.

Serves 4–6

1 4-pound first-cut brisket of beef
6 cloves garlic, 3 cut into slivers and 3
    crushed
4 large onions, thinly sliced
1 cup cider vinegar
1½ tablespoons bacon fat
1 cup strong black coffee
Salt and freshly ground pepper to taste
½ cup water

1. With a long, thin, sharp knife, make slits in the meat and insert the slivers of garlic. Place the meat in a bowl, spread 1 sliced onion and the crushed garlic over the meat, and pour in the vinegar. Marinate for 6 hours at room temperature or overnight in the refrigerator, turning the meat several times.

2. Preheat oven to 350° F.

3. Heat the bacon fat in a deep, heavy skillet large enough to hold the brisket. Remove the brisket from the marinade and discard the onion and vinegar. Dry with paper towels. Brown the meat well on all sides.

4. Remove the brisket to a platter. In the fat remaining in the skillet, sauté the remaining sliced onions until deeply browned. Pour in ½ cup of the coffee. Bring to a boil, stirring and scraping the bottom of the skillet to loosen the browned bits.

5. Spread the onions and liquid from the skillet in a shallow baking dish. Place the brisket on the onions. Season with salt and pepper. Pour in the remaining coffee and water. Cover tightly with foil and place in oven for ½ hour.

6. Turn oven down to 250° F. and bake for an additional 2 hours or until meat is very tender.

7. Slice the brisket thinly against the grain. Skim the fat from the pan liquid. Return the meat slices to the pan. Serve at once, or refrigerate for later use.

BRAISED PORK CHOPS WITH CHESTNUTS AND MUSHROOMS

🧄Chestnuts, already peeled and cooked, are available in cans (they must be rinsed) or jars (no rinsing needed) in gourmet shops or in the gourmet departments of some supermarkets. Cook the chops until they are *just* done, so that they remain juicy. Cut into one at the bone. It should exhibit just the faintest blush of pink. This is a very festive winter dish.

Serves 4–6

Flour
Salt and freshly ground pepper to taste
6 pork chops, about ¾ inch thick, trimmed
    of fat
2 tablespoons unsalted butter
2 tablespoons corn oil
¼ cup plus 3 tablespoons applejack or Calva-
    dos
½ cup dry vermouth
½ teaspoon dried thyme
½ teaspoon unsalted butter
½ cup sliced scallions
½ pound small mushrooms, cleaned,
    trimmed, and halved
¾ cup cooked chestnuts, quartered

¼ cup chicken stock
Glazed Onions and Garlic (recipe follows)
Chopped fresh parsley

1. Spread flour on a sheet of waxed paper. Season with salt and pepper.

2. Dry the chops. Dredge them in the seasoned flour, shaking off the excess.

3. Heat the butter and oil in a wide, heavy skillet. Brown the chops, without crowding, in the hot fat, a minute or two on each side. Remove to a platter. Pour out fat from skillet.

4. Pour in ¼ cup of the applejack or Calvados and bring to a boil. Stand back and avert your face—the brandy might flame. Pour in ¼ cup of the vermouth and let boil for a minute or two.

5. Put the pork chops back in the skillet in one layer. Sprinkle in the thyme. Cover and simmer, turning occasionally, for about ½ hour or until tender and just cooked through. (Do not let them get dried out.) Remove the chops to a platter and keep warm. The liquid will have cooked away and the chops will be quite brown.

6. Add the ½ teaspoon butter to the skillet and melt. Sauté the scallions and mushrooms, tossing them in the skillet, until the scallions are soft.

7. Pour in the remaining 3 tablespoons applejack and ¼ cup vermouth. Bring to a boil, stirring and scraping the bottom of the skillet with a wooden spoon to loosen the encrusted bits. Add the chestnuts and the stock and boil until the stock forms a dark, rich, thick sauce—only a minute or so.

8. Heap the glazed onions and garlic in the middle of an attractive platter. Overlap the chops in a circle around the onions and garlic. Spoon some mushroom-chestnut sauce over each chop, sprinkle with parsley, and serve at once.

Glazed Onions and Garlic

2 tablespoons unsalted butter
1 pound pearl onions, boiled for 3 minutes
    and peeled
60 cloves garlic, parboiled and peeled
1 tablespoon sugar
¼ cup water

1. Melt the butter in a wide, heavy skillet. Spread the onions and garlic in the skillet in one layer and cook, shaking pan occasionally so that the onions and garlic are tossed in the hot fat for a few minutes.

2. Sprinkle the onions and garlic with sugar, and continue to cook over moderate heat, shaking the pan frequently to ensure even browning.

3. When the onions and garlic have caramelized and turned amber, pour in the water to dissolve the caramelized bits adhering to the skillet. Shake and cook until the liquid is almost gone and the onions and garlic are tender and beautifully brown.

GARLIC WINE

One of the oddest products to grow out of Gilroy, California's, annual garlic festival was a special wine. Gilroy's Rapazzini Winery introduced its grape wine flavored with garlic with daring flamboyance in 1983. "Garlic Wine," states the label. "A unique experience that will never leave you breathless." The *Chicago Sun Times* described it as "a vintage with a light amber color and what you might call a good nose, if you like garlic." Rapazzini's new wine is *the* wine to drink with the recipes in this book, and it makes an excellent cooking wine for any recipe calling for dry white wine or vermouth. The garlic flavor hovers in the background, a subtle accent to the good flinty taste of the grape.

FLANK STEAK WITH GARLIC WINE SAUCE

🧄 This method of cooking and saucing beef will work with any cut of steak—filet, rib eye, sirloin, etc. I like flank steak because it has little waste and excellent flavor and texture.

Serves 4

1 well-trimmed flank steak, about 1½ pounds
Salt and freshly ground pepper to taste
4 tablespoons unsalted butter, 2 softened
2 tablespoons thinly sliced scallions
1 cup dry red wine
Purée from 1 large head Roasted Garlic (see pages 14-15)

1. Sprinkle flank steak with salt and a generous amount of freshly ground black pepper.

2. Heat a wide, heavy skillet. Do not add fat. When hot, cook seasoned steak until seared and well browned on each side (about 1 minute per side).

3. Reduce heat and add 2 tablespoons butter. Cook 3 to 5 minutes on each side. For best results, the meat should remain quite rare.

4. Remove the meat from the pan and keep warm. Pour off the fat in the skillet and add the scallions and red wine. Bring to a boil and whisk in the garlic purée. Boil until the wine is reduced by half, thickened, and syrupy. As it boils, scrape up the browned particles in the skillet with a wooden spoon. Stir in the meat juices that have accumulated under the flank steak. Boil for 1 or 2 seconds more.

5. Remove from the heat. Gently swirl in the 2 tablespoons softened butter so that it incorporates into the wine.

6. Quickly slice the meat, against the grain, into thin strips. Arrange the slices on a hot platter, pour sauce down the center of them, and serve at once.

> "What do you think? Young women of rank actually eat—you will never guess what—garlick! Our poor friend Lord Byron is quite corrupted by living among these people."
> **SHELLEY**
> **in a letter from Naples, 1818**

PORK STEAKS WITH LIME

❧ Unlike pork chops, pork shoulder steaks must be braised slowly to become tender. Here the pork is braised in a Southwestern combination of tomato, lime, garlic, and chili. This dish can be made a day or so ahead and reheated.

Serves 6

2 tablespoons unsalted butter
1 tablespoon vegetable oil
6 pork shoulder steaks, about ¾ inch thick
Salt and freshly ground pepper to taste
1 large onion, cut in half and sliced into
    paper-thin half moons
3 or 4 small chili peppers (more or less to
    taste), rinsed, stemmed, seeded, and
    chopped
1 can (1 pound 12 ounces) plum tomatoes,
    drained and crushed with the hands
40 cloves garlic, parboiled and peeled
1 tablespoon chopped fresh parsley
3 tablespoons dark-brown sugar
2 limes, sliced paper-thin

1. Preheat oven to 300° F.

2. Heat the butter and oil in a wide, heavy casserole that can be used on top of the stove and in the oven.

3. Trim the steaks of surrounding fat. Sprinkle with salt and pepper. Sauté until nicely browned on both sides. Transfer to a platter.

4. In the fat remaining in the casserole, sauté the onions until browned. Stir and scrape the bottom of the casserole as you sauté to loosen the browned bits. Stir in the chili peppers. Heap the onions and peppers on the platter next to the steaks.

5. Pour the tomatoes into the casserole. Scatter in the garlic cloves. Season with salt and pepper. Bring to a simmer and cook, stirring occasionally, for 5 to 7 minutes. Stir in the parsley.

6. Place the steaks, in a single layer, on the tomatoes. Heap the onions between the steaks. Sprinkle ½ tablespoon of dark-brown sugar over each steak. Cover each steak with slices of lime.

7. Cover the casserole tightly, with foil if necessary, and bake in the oven for 1 to 1½ hours or until the meat is very tender.

BRAISED BEEF ROLL STUFFED WITH VEAL PATE

🧄🧄 The slices of pâté-stuffed beef and the red sauce make a lusty, very attractive dish. It is quite good served cold.

Serves 6–8

1 large well-trimmed flank steak (2 pounds if possible)
Freshly ground pepper to taste
1 pound ground veal
1 egg, lightly beaten
¼ cup bread crumbs
4 tablespoons freshly ground Parmesan cheese
1 cup plus 3 tablespoons chopped fresh parsley
1 teaspoon dried basil or 1 tablespoon chopped fresh
6 thin slices prosciutto
4 ounces provolone cheese, cut into 1-inch strips
24 cloves garlic, 20 parboiled and peeled, 4 minced
¼ cup plus 3 tablespoons olive oil
2 large onions, chopped
2 large cans (1 pound 12 ounces each) plum tomatoes, drained and chopped
1 6-ounce can of tomato paste
1 bay leaf
½ teaspoon dried basil

Salt and freshly ground pepper to taste
1 cup dry red wine
Beef stock

1. Butterfly the flank steak as follows: slit it down the long end with a very sharp knife; cut it very carefully almost all the way through until you can open it flat like a book.

2. On your work surface, spread out the butterflied steak on a sheet of waxed paper. Sprinkle with freshly ground pepper. Cover with another sheet of waxed paper. Pound the steak gently with a kitchen mallet or the side of a wide knife, until it is about ¼ inch thick. Set aside.

3. In a bowl, combine the veal, egg, bread crumbs, Parmesan cheese, 3 tablespoons parsley, basil, and salt and pepper; use your hands or a wooden spoon to mix it very well. Set aside.

4. Lay the slices of prosciutto over the surface of the butterflied flank steak. Spread the veal stuffing over it. Place the strips of provolone over the stuffing, pushing them in. In a similar fashion, push in the 20 parboiled garlic cloves. Starting from the long edge of the flank, roll it up like a jelly roll into a long sausagelike shape. Tie the roll securely crosswise in several places with kitchen string. Secure both ends with wooden toothpicks and tie it once lengthwise.

5. Heat ¼ cup olive oil in a wide, heavy skillet. Dry the beef with paper towels. Brown it well on all sides in the hot oil, using tongs to turn it.

6. Meanwhile, prepare the sauce. Heat 3 tablespoons olive oil in a deep pot that can be covered and is large enough to hold the beef roll. Cook the onions and the minced garlic in the hot oil until limp. Add the tomatoes, tomato paste, bay leaf, basil, salt and pepper. Bring to a boil, then reduce to a simmer.

7. Preheat oven to 325° F.

8. When the beef is thoroughly browned, put it in the pot with the tomato mixture. Drain the oil out of the skillet and pour in the red wine. Bring the wine to a boil, and boil for 2 to 3 minutes, scraping up the browned particles on the bottom of the skillet with a wooden spoon. Pour the wine into the pot with the beef. Add enough stock so that the sauce comes almost to the top of the beef roll. Simmer, covered, in the oven for 1 to 1½ hours, until the beef is tender. Adjust oven temperature during this time, so that the contents of the pot remain at a simmer.

9. When done, remove the meat and let it stand for 5 to 10 minutes. Skim the fat from the sauce. Cut the string from the beef and discard. Carve the beef roll into ½-inch slices and arrange on a platter. Spoon some sauce down the center of each slice and sprinkle with parsley. Serve the rest of the sauce separately.

GARLIC HOME REMEDIES

One very popular cure for both worms and the common cold was to apply a poultice of crushed raw garlic to the soles of the feet. A patient who went to bed with garlic feet woke up with garlic breath, ample proof that the garlic was working. This method was used to treat bad coughs, too, even whooping cough! A whole clove was sometimes used as a suppository for a host of digestive ills, and crushed garlic rubbed vigorously where it would do the most good was believed to be just the thing to increase male sexual potency.

Earaches were treated by a split clove of garlic either rubbed on and around the ailing ear or placed inside the ear, and toothaches, by the insertion of garlic slivers into the troublesome cavity. One folk remedy advocated curing toothaches simply by clutching garlic cloves firmly in the hand. Various North American Indian tribes used garlic to relieve insect stings and bites, and many cultures have used raw cloves as a topical acne treatment. To this very day, on the Sea Islands of Georgia and North Carolina, some Gullahs (descendants of black African slaves, who have preserved their culture to a remarkable degree) wear cloves of garlic around the neck in the belief that such a necklace will prevent high blood pressure.

GARLIC CARNITAS

🧄These marvelous tidbits are delicious served with guacamole and *salsa fria*. Serve with toothpicks as a first course. Let diners mash the garlic so it pops out of its skin and dunk the meat into the sauces and garlic or—best of all—serve as a main course and let the diners combine the meat, two sauces, and garlic to taste.

Serves 6–8

3 pounds pork butt, trimmed of all thick outside fat and boned (weight after trimming and boning)
25 large garlic cloves, unpeeled
Salt and freshly ground pepper to taste
Salsa Fria (recipe follows)
Guacamole (recipe follows)

1. Preheat oven to 350° F.

2. Cut meat into 1-inch chunks. Mix meat cubes and garlic cloves. Spread out in one layer in a shallow baking dish. Bake, uncovered, for 25 minutes.

3. Remove the dish from the oven. If the meat has released a quantity of liquid, drain it away. Season the meat and garlic generously with salt and pepper. Stir the meat around in the dish and spread it out again so that it remains in one layer. Bake for an additional 35 minutes, until the garlic is tender and brown and the meat cubes are browned outside and just done and juicy inside. Do not overcook or the meat will dry out. Serve very hot with guacamole and *salsa fria*.

Salsa Fria

Makes approximately 5 cups

4 cups tomatoes, peeled, seeded, and chopped (if ripe tomatoes are unavailable, use canned tomatoes)
¼ cup canned chopped green chilies, drained
¼ cup red wine vinegar
2 tablespoons olive oil
2 cloves garlic, minced
2 tablespoons fresh parsley, chopped
1 tablespoon coriander leaves, chopped
1 tablespoon fresh oregano, chopped (½ teaspoon dried)
1 teaspoon fresh thyme, chopped (¼ teaspoon dried)
1 tablespoon fresh basil, chopped (½ teaspoon dried)
Salt and freshly ground pepper to taste

Combine all the ingredients in a nonreactive (see page 10) bowl. Chill. Serve with *carnitas* or as a dip with tortilla chips.

Guacamole

Makes approximately 4 cups

2 large, ripe avocados
Juice of 1 lime
2–3 canned green chilies, peeled and chopped
Several dashes Tabasco sauce
2 tablespoons mild onion, finely minced
1 large ripe tomato, peeled, seeded, juiced,
    and finely chopped

2–3 sprigs chopped fresh coriander
Salt and freshly ground pepper to taste

1. Cut the avocados in half and remove the pits. Scoop out the flesh into a bowl. With a fork, mash the avocado with the lime juice.

2. Add the remaining ingredients and mash well. The mixture should be a rough purée. Serve with *carnitas*. Prepare this just before serving or it will turn dark. (Good with tortilla chips or raw vegetables dippers, too.)

LEMONY LAMB CHOPS

🧄🧄 This makes an easy-to-prepare family supper. The shoulder chops, in their lemony, garlicky bath, are satisfying and warming.

Serves 4–6

3 tablespoons vegetable oil
6 shoulder lamb chops, ¾ inch thick
Salt and freshly ground pepper to taste
1 large onion, cut in half and sliced into thin
    half moons
6 cloves garlic, minced
1 cup fresh lemon juice
1 cup chicken stock
1 bay leaf
Grated rind of 1 lemon

1. Preheat oven to 300° F.

2. Heat the oil in a casserole or baking dish that will hold the chops in one layer and can be used both on the stove and in the oven.

3. Trim the chops of surrounding fat. Sprinkle with salt and pepper.

4. Sear the chops on both sides in the hot oil. Remove to a platter and keep warm.

5. Add the onions and garlic and cook until limp, adding more oil if necessary. When limp, drain off any excess oil.

6. Stir in the remaining ingredients. Bring to a boil, scraping the bottom of the casserole with a wooden spoon to loosen browned bits.

7. Return the chops to the casserole. Cover the pan tightly, with foil if necessary. Bake in the preheated oven for 45 minutes to 1 hour, until the chops are fork-tender. Skim the fat from the pan juices and serve.

LAMB-MATZOH DUMPLINGS WITH EGGPLANT-GARLIC JAM

The eggplant-garlic jam is a variation of "poor man's caviar" (Is there a rich man's eggplant made with caviar?) and is loaded with garlic purée; the lamb dumplings are laced with fresh ginger. As you dip a dumpling into the jam and take a bite, the two flavors play against each other in a most exhilarating way. Make the jam well in advance, as it will keep for a week or more and improve in flavor as it waits. Leave out for ½ hour or so before serving, so that it is not ice cold. The jam is also delicious served as a first course with black bread or with matzoh.

Serves 6

2 pounds ground lamb
1 cup unsalted matzoh meal
4 eggs
Salt and freshly ground pepper to taste
½ teaspoon ground cumin
½ teaspoon ground cinnamon
Juice of 1 lemon
Grated rind of 1 lemon
1 piece fresh ginger, 2 inches long, finely peeled and grated
½ cup chopped fresh parsley
Vegetable oil
3 cups chicken stock
Eggplant-Garlic Jam (recipe follows)

1. Combine the lamb, matzoh meal, eggs, seasonings, lemon juice and rind, ginger, and parsley in a bowl. Mix well with the hands. Fry a tiny piece in a small skillet. Taste and adjust seasonings to your liking.

2. Form the mixture into small balls (about the size of walnuts). Film a large, heavy skillet with vegetable oil to a depth of ⅛ inch. Heat.

3. Sauté the dumplings (do them in batches and do not crowd them) in the skillet until they are browned and crusty on the outside and *just* cooked through (about 5 to 7 minutes for each batch). Shake the pan to expose all sides of the dumplings to the hot oil. Replace oil as needed.

4. As they are done, transfer the dumplings to a paper-towel-lined plate and blot well. When all are drained and blotted, spread them in a wide, shallow dish in layers, cover with plastic wrap, and refrigerate until needed. They will keep for 3 to 4 days.

5. To heat and serve, pour the chicken stock into a pot and bring to a boil. Add the lamb dumplings and simmer gently for 5 to 10 minutes, until heated through. Remove with a slotted spoon and arrange on a platter. Serve each diner a few dumplings and a dollop of eggplant-garlic jam.

Eggplant-Garlic Jam

4 medium eggplants
Salt
Olive oil
Juice of 1 large lemon
1 can (1 pound 12 ounces) tomatoes, drained, seeded, and crushed
Purée from two heads Roasted Garlic (see pages 14-15)
Salt and freshly ground pepper to taste
¼ cup chopped parsley
¼ cup pine nuts

1. Preheat oven to 400° F.

2. Cut eggplants in half lengthwise. Salt cut sides liberally and place upside down on a stainless-steel rack to drain for ½ hour. Then rinse and dry with paper towels.

3. Brush the cut sides of eggplant with olive oil and place them, cut-side up, on a lightly oiled baking sheet (or 2 sheets, if the sheets are small). Bake the eggplant for 50 to 60 minutes, until soft, collapsed, and browned.

4. Scrape the soft eggplant flesh out of the skins into a colander. Allow to drain for 10 minutes and discard the skins.

5. Force the eggplant pulp through a sieve, to remove the seeds.

6. Place the pulp in the bowl of an electric mixer. Beat in all the remaining ingredients.

7. Scrape the jam into a bowl, cover, and refrigerate.

ROASTED ITALIAN SAUSAGE AND POTATOES WITH WHOLE GARLIC CLOVES

♣ This is the sort of earthy, simple combination of foods I love: browned, tender little potatoes, spicy sausages that are cracklingly crisp on the outside and juicy within, and cloves of soft, sweet garlic. Serve it with beer or a hearty red wine and a salad of strong greens.

Serves 6-8

24 small new potatoes, unpeeled and halved
2 large onions, peeled and quartered
25 large cloves garlic, unpeeled
Salt and freshly ground pepper to taste
12 links Italian sausage—hot, sweet, or a
    combination of both
¼ cup water
Chopped fresh parsley

1. Preheat oven to 400° F.

2. Spread the potatoes, onions, and garlic in a shallow baking dish wide enough to hold them in one layer. Season with salt and pepper.

3. Place a rack over the baking dish. Prick each sausage with a thin skewer, and arrange on the rack. Roast in the preheated oven for 45 minutes to 1 hour or until the sausages are browned and just done (don't dry them out) and the potatoes are tender. During the baking time, stir up the potatoes and turn the sausages once.

4. When done, set the sausages aside and keep warm. With a slotted spoon, remove the potatoes, onions, and garlic cloves to a platter. Pour off and discard fat from baking dish. Pour in ¼ cup water. Bring to a boil on top of the stove, scraping up the baked-on meat juices with a wooden spoon. Pour the liquid over potatoes, top with the sausages, and sprinkle with chopped parsley. Serve at once. Each diner should press down on the garlic cloves with a fork so that the soft insides pop out, to be eaten with the potatoes and sausage.

MIDDLE EASTERN BEANS WITH LAMB SAUCE

🧄🧄Sometimes it's fun to sauce vegetables as if they were a form of pasta. Cook the beans a little beyond the crisp-tender stage. This is delicious reheated. Garnish with yogurt just before serving.

Serves 6

1½ pounds ground lamb
2 onions, coarsely chopped
4 cloves garlic, crushed
1 can (1 pound 12 ounces) tomatoes, chopped
1 12-ounce can tomato purée
Salt and freshly ground pepper to taste
1 teaspoon cinnamon
½ teaspoon nutmeg
Juice of 1 lemon
2 pounds green beans, trimmed
1½ cups plain yogurt, drained for 6–7 hours as described in *Tzatziki* recipe (see page 33)
Fresh mint leaves, chopped

1. In a wide, deep, heavy skillet, sauté the lamb, onions, and garlic. (Add no fat—the lamb will cook in its own fat.) As it cooks, break up the lumps of meat with a wooden spoon. When the meat is cooked and the onions and garlic are tender, drain well in a colander to eliminate all the rendered fat. Return meat mixture to skillet.

2. Add the tomatoes and their juices, tomato purée, seasonings, and lemon juice. Bring to a boil, reduce heat, and simmer, partially covered, until the sauce is thick. Stir occasionally during this time. Taste and adjust seasonings, adding salt, pepper, and lemon juice as needed.

3. Meanwhile, steam the beans over boiling water until tender.

4. Serve the beans in shallow bowls topped with the piping hot sauce, a generous dollop of cold drained yogurt, and a sprinkling of mint.

"Make your conversation a kissing-sweet experience."
Rapazzini wine label, 1983

BRAISED LEG OF LAMB ARLESIENNE

♣♣ This Provençal leg of lamb, from cookbook-author, garlic lover Perla Meyers, is so tender that it can be eaten with a spoon. The lamb may be cooked hours in advance and reheated in the pan juices in a low oven or over low heat on top of the stove.

Serves 6

1 leg of lamb, about 6½ pounds, boned and rolled
Salt and freshly ground black pepper
1 teaspoon dried marjoram
2 tablespoons finely minced fresh rosemary (or 1 teaspoon dried)
2 tablespoons finely minced fresh thyme (or 1 teaspoon dried)
52 large cloves garlic, 2 peeled and finely crushed, 50 parboiled and peeled
2 tablespoons fruity olive oil
1 tablespoon unsalted butter
¼ cup Armagnac or Cognac
1 cup dry white wine
1¼ cups stock
2 medium onions, peeled and quartered
2 teaspoons cornstarch, mixed with a little stock
Sprigs of fresh parsley

1. Preheat oven to 350° F.

2. Dry the meat thoroughly with paper towels. Season with salt and pepper, then rub with marjoram, rosemary, and thyme. Make tiny slits in the meat and insert pieces of the crushed garlic. Set aside.

3. In a heavy oval casserole, heat the oil and butter. When the fat is very hot, add the roast and brown on all sides over medium heat. Add the Armagnac or Cognac, spooning it over the meat, and cook, turning the meat until all the brandy has evaporated.

4. Add the wine and bring to a boil. Add ½ cup of the stock, the onions, and the parboiled garlic. Cover the casserole with foil and then top with the lid (the casserole must be tightly covered). Set in the center of the oven.

5. Braise the lamb for 3½ hours, basting it with the pan juices every 15 to 20 minutes. Adjust the temperature during the cooking so that contents of pot remain at a simmer, not a boil. When the lamb is done, transfer it carefully to a deep serving platter. It will be very tender and can easily fall apart. Remove the strings and set it aside.

6. Carefully degrease the pan juices, leaving the onions and garlic in the casserole.

7. Place the casserole over medium heat and add the remaining stock. Bring to a boil and whisk in a little of the cornstarch mixture; use just enough to thicken the sauce. Taste the sauce and correct the seasoning.

8. Spoon the sauce over the lamb and garnish with sprigs of parsley. Serve with a side dish of a potato-and-turnip purée or a gratin of potatoes and a well-seasoned green salad.

GARLIC-STUFFED PORK ROAST

This roast, and the stock and port that it is roasted with, produce a marvelous thick brown gravy.

Serves 6

1 pork shoulder roast (Boston butt), boned, trimmed of top fat, and butterflied, about 4 pounds
Salt and freshly ground pepper to taste
5 cloves garlic, coarsley chopped
3 heaping tablespoons freshly grated Parmesan cheese
20 sprigs parsley, trimmed of stems (save stems for a future stock)
2 tablespoons pine nuts
Stock
Dry white port

1. Preheat oven to 325° F.

2. Spread the butterflied pork roast flat on your work surface, boned-side up. With a sharp knife, score the top surface in several places. Sprinkle with salt and a generous amount of freshly ground pepper.

3. Sprinkle the garlic, cheese, parsley, and pine nuts over the meat. Roll the roast and tie it securely in several places.

4. Place the meat on a rack in a shallow roasting pan. Pour in ¼ cup stock and ¼ cup port. Begin roasting in the preheated oven.

5. When the liquid in the pan is almost gone and beginning to leave an encrustation on the bottom of the pan, replenish with more stock and a splash of port. Continue roasting until done, replenishing stock and wine as needed. It will cook about 2¼ hours in all. (It is done when a meat thermometer registers a temperature of 170° F.)

6. Remove the roast to a cutting board and let it rest for 10 minutes. Skim the pan juices of as much fat as possible.

7. Strain the liquid into the roasting pan and bring to a boil on top of the stove. Boil rapidly for 2 or 3 minutes until thick and syrupy, scraping up the browned bits and encrustations on the pan as the liquid boils.

8. Remove strings from roast and slice. Arrange on a platter and serve. Serve the pan juices separately.

TRANSYLVANIAN GOULASH

♣♣This heavenly combination of pork, sauerkraut, and sour cream might have been Count Dracula's favorite dish. But, as my 11-year-old son pointed out, 5 cloves of garlic keep the goulash from becoming "ghoulash"; any vampire worth his fangs could not tolerate even a whiff. Prepare this dish a few days in advance for maximum flavor.

Serves 6

3 pounds fresh sauerkraut
6 slices bacon, diced
3 onions, coarsley chopped
5 cloves garlic, crushed
4 tablespoons sweet Hungarian paprika
1 tablespoon hot Hungarian paprika (or use a total of 5 tablespoons sweet paprika and cayenne pepper to taste)
2 tablespoons caraway seeds
1 large can (1 pound 12 ounces) tomatoes, drained and chopped
Salt and freshly ground pepper to taste
3 pounds well-trimmed pork shoulder, cut into 1-inch cubes
1½–2 cups chicken stock
2 tablespoons flour
1 cup sour cream, at room temperature

1. Drain the sauerkraut in a colander. Rinse it well in cold water, then drain and squeeze as dry as possible. (Save the juice for drinking. It's reputed to be just the thing for bad hangovers.) Set aside.

2. Slowly cook the diced bacon in a deep, heavy pot that can be covered. When the bacon is not quite crisp, remove it with a slotted spoon and set it aside.

3. Add the onions and garlic to the bacon fat. Cook slowly until limp but not brown.

4. Add the paprika and stir over very low heat until the onions and garlic are well coated. Stir in the caraway seeds and reserved bacon.

5. Add the tomatoes, salt, pepper, pork, and sauerkraut. Toss gently to combine.

6. Pour in enough stock to barely cover the contents of pot. Bring to a simmer, cover, and cook over very low heat for about 1½ hours or until pork is tender.

7. With a wire whisk, stir the flour into the sour cream. Stir a bit of the hot liquid from the pot into the sour cream, then pour the sour cream mixture back into the goulash, stirring constantly. Simmer for an additional 10 minutes, stirring occasionally.

Pasta

"There is no such thing as a little garlic."
ARTHUR BAER, 1886

PASTA WITH TOMATO-GARLIC SAUCE

🧄This recipe and the simple variation that follows are the work of Joseph deAssereto, chef/owner of the splendid Washington, D.C., Italian restaurant, Cantina D'Italia. I first learned of it through National Public Radio's "All Things Considered." Anchorwoman Susan Stamberg kept up a running commentary as she twirled the pasta onto her fork and began to eat. "And what are these—scallops?" she asked as she began to nibble on the garlic. "No, whole garlic cloves," replied de Assereto, and his answer hung there, for a moment, until the conversation abruptly turned to the question of using a spoon or not to facilitate twirling pasta on a fork. Here is proof of the mysterious and subtle taste of simmered, whole cloves. Your guests will nibble happily at the cloves and ask, "Scallops? Blanched almonds? Lobster nuggets?" They'll never know the truth until you tell.

Serves 4–6

60 cloves garlic, parboiled and peeled
Chicken stock
1 cup olive oil
½ cup chopped onions
1 teaspoon diced fresh red chilies
6 fresh tomatoes, peeled, seeded, and diced
Salt and freshly ground pepper to taste
1 cup fresh basil leaves
1 tablespoon tomato paste
¾–1 pound fettucine
Parmesan cheese

1. Boil the peeled garlic cloves in stock to cover for about 15 minutes, until tender. Drain and set aside.

2. Heat the olive oil in a wide, heavy skillet. Sauté the onions until golden.

3. Add the hot peppers and sauté a few moments more. Add the tomatoes and salt and pepper to taste. When the mixture is bubbling, add the basil, garlic, and tomato paste. Mix well and heat through.

4. Cook the fettucine to the *al dente* stage. Drain. Toss with garlic-tomato sauce and serve at once. Serve freshly grated Parmesan cheese at the table.

LINGUINE WITH EGGPLANT-SAUSAGE SAUCE

♣♣Well-made Italian sausage is a favorite of mine. Combined with eggplant, plenty of garlic, green peppers, and tomatoes, it makes a substantial and lovely sauce for linguine.

Serves 4–6

1 medium eggplant
Salt
3 tablespoons olive oil
3 tablespoons unsalted butter
1 large onion, coarsely diced
1 pound Italian sausage, sweet or hot,
    skinned and broken into pieces
3 tablespoons chopped fresh parsley
3 green peppers, halved, trimmed, and thinly
    sliced
4 cloves garlic, minced
1 16-ounce can tomatoes, drained and
    rubbed through a sieve
4 large ripe tomatoes, peeled, seeded, juiced,
    and diced
Salt and freshly ground pepper to taste
¾–1 pound linguine, cooked *al dente*
Freshly grated Parmesan cheese

1. Trim the eggplant, but do not peel it. Dice it into ½-inch cubes. Place in a nonreactive (see page 10) bowl and salt liberally. Let stand to sweat for ½ hour. Rinse, drain, and dry thoroughly on paper towels.

2. Heat the olive oil and butter in a deep skillet. Sauté the onion gently until very tender and lightly browned.

3. Toss in the sausage and cook gently, stirring occasionally, for 10 minutes. Add the parsley and cook for 10 minutes more.

4. Toss in the eggplant cubes, green pepper slices, and garlic. Cook, tossing and turning the vegetables in the skillet, for 5 minutes.

5. Stir in the sieved canned tomatoes and diced fresh tomatoes. Season to taste with salt and pepper. Bring to a simmer. Simmer, uncovered, stirring occasionally for 15 minutes. Serve with linguine and plenty of grated Parmesan.

"**That wicked garlic, more poisonous than the hemlock...**"

HORACE
Episode 3

CALIFORNIA PASTA PRIMAVERA

♣♣Don't be frightened by the number of steps in this glorious summer pasta dish from the Fresh Garlic Association. Each component is simply made, and when combined, the whole thing is a crunchy, creamy, zesty vegetarian symphony.

Serves 6–8

2½ cups broccoli flowerets
12 stalks asparagus, trimmed of tough areas, peeled up to the buds, and cut into thirds
1 medium zucchini, sliced
½ pound green beans, cut into 1-inch lengths
1½ cups snow pea pods
2 tablespoons olive oil
3 cups sliced mushrooms
⅓ cup pine nuts
1 pound thin spaghetti
Red Sauce (recipe follows)
Cream Sauce (recipe follows)

1. Steam each vegetable except mushrooms separately over boiling water until barely crisp-tender. This will take from 30 seconds to 5 minutes, depending on the vegetable. Do not let them get overcooked and flaccid.

2. As soon as each is cooked, cool it under cold running water.

3. Drain and set aside until needed.

4. Heat oil in a large skillet.

5. Toss the mushrooms and pine nuts in the hot oil until golden.

6. Cover and keep warm until needed.

7. Cook spaghetti in boiling salted water, *al dente*.

8. While the pasta is cooking, turn heat on under mushrooms and pine nuts.

9. When hot, toss in the steamed vegetables and cook for 4 to 5 minutes, stirring until hot.

10. Turn up heat under the two sauces.

11. Drain the spaghetti.

12. Toss with the cream sauce. Add ⅔ of the vegetable mixture and toss again.

13. Top with the remaining vegetables and red sauce.

14. Serve at once.

Red Sauce

3 tablespoons olive oil
3 cups peeled, seeded, juiced, and cubed ripe tomatoes
¼ cup chopped fresh parsley (Italian if possible)

2 tablespoons chopped fresh basil
6 cloves garlic, finely minced
Salt and freshly ground pepper to taste

1. Heat the oil in a skillet.

2. Add the remaining red sauce ingredients.

3. Cook for 4 minutes, stirring, until hot.

4. Cover and keep warm until needed.

Cream Sauce

¼ pound (1 stick) unsalted butter
1 cup whipping cream
1 cup grated Parmesan cheese
Salt and freshly ground pepper to taste
6 tablespoons chopped fresh basil

1. Melt the butter in a saucepan.

2. Stir in the remaining ingredients, stirring until smooth and hot.

3. Keep warm until needed.

PASTA WITH GARLIC SAUCE, CANTINA D'ITALIA

Serves 4–6

60 cloves garlic, parboiled and peeled
Chicken stock
1 cup olive oil
2 teaspoons diced fresh hot red peppers
1 cup fresh basil leaves
Salt and freshly ground pepper to taste
¾–1 pound fettucine
Grated Parmesan cheese

1. Boil the peeled garlic cloves in stock to cover for about 15 minutes, until tender. Drain and set aside.

2. Heat the olive oil in a wide, heavy skillet. Add the peppers and garlic and heat through. Season with salt and pepper, and stir in the basil leaves.

3. Serve over freshly cooked, *al dente* fettucine. Serve the Parmesan cheese at the table.

PASTA WITH MARINATED TOMATO SAUCE

This is blissful in very much the way as a hot fudge sundae. The hot pasta and the cold sauce mingle together on the tongue in a wonderful confusion of contrasts. Don't even think of making this with pallid supermarket tomatoes or with canned tomatoes. Make it in the summer and use the ripest, juiciest tomatoes you can find.

Serves 4–6

12 ripe tomatoes, peeled, seeded, and juiced
3 large cloves garlic, crushed
½ cup chopped fresh parsley
¼ cup scallions, thinly sliced
¼ cup chopped fresh basil
2 tablespoons capers
¾ cup black Greek or Niçoise olives, halved and pitted
6 tablespoons olive oil
2 tablespoons wine vinegar
Salt and freshly ground pepper to taste
¾–1 pound linguine or fettucine, cooked *al dente*

1. Dice the tomatoes coarsely. Combine in a nonreactive (see page 10) bowl with all the remaining ingredients, except the pasta. Let marinate for an hour or so.

2. Dump the hot, freshly cooked and drained pasta into a warm bowl. Top with the sauce and serve at once.

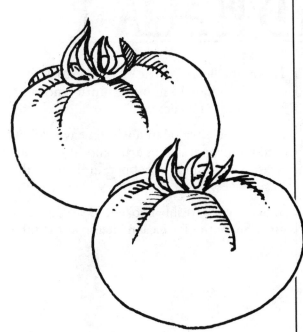

ANDREA SMITH'S PASTA WITH CLAMS

🧄🧄 Andy Smith is a food consultant in Atlanta. Her recipe for vermicelli and clams is livened up with plenty of garlic and oily black olives.

Serves 6

3 dozen fresh clams (allow 5–6 clams per person)
½ pound unsalted butter
¼ cup chopped fresh parsley
6–8 cloves garlic, minced
12–15 pitted, Greek or Niçoise black olives, chopped
1 pound vermicelli
Salt
Olive oil
Freshly ground black pepper

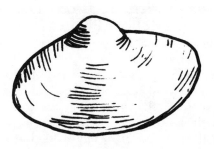

1. To prepare clams, soak them in a bowl of lightly salted water. Scrub the shells with a brush to remove grit and sand. Discard any clams with open or broken shells. To test for live clams, sharply tap shell. If shells do not tightly shut, discard.

2. Place a small amount of water in a pot, add a pinch of salt, and bring to a boil. Add the clams, cover, and steam for approximately 6 to 10 minutes, or until clam shells open.

3. To make the sauce, melt ½ stick of the butter in a skillet. Add the parsley and garlic and cook for 1 minute. Add the remaining butter, allow it to melt, remove the skillet from the heat, and add the olives.

4. To prepare the pasta, bring a large pot of water to a boil. Add salt and olive oil. Feed the noodles into the water, being careful not to break the pasta strands. Simmer until *al dente,* strain, and rinse with hot water.

5. To serve, drain the vermicelli, add half of the sauce, and toss well. Season with pepper. Top with the clams in their shells and cover with the remaining sauce.

MACARONI-CHEESE CUSTARD

♣This is a very flossy version of macaroni and cheese. The pasta shells are nestled in a creamy, garlic-scented, scallion-studded, cheese-strewn custard. Cut it in wedges to serve.

Serves 6

4 ounces pasta shells, uncooked
1 tablespoon unsalted butter
5 scallions, sliced
2 large eggs
1 cup ricotta cheese
1 cup half-and-half
6 tablespoons Parmesan cheese
Purée from 1 head Roasted Garlic (see pages 14-15)
1 tablespoon Dijon mustard
Salt and freshly ground pepper to taste
½ teaspoon dried tarragon, crumbled
½ cup grated Gruyère cheese

1. Preheat oven to 350° F.

2. Cook the pasta; it should be somewhat undercooked, because it will bake in the custard later on. Drain it in a colander, rinse it in cold water, and drain it again.

3. Heat the butter in a small skillet. Sauté the scallions until tender.

4. Beat the eggs with the ricotta cheese in a large bowl. Beat in the half-and-half, Parmesan, garlic, mustard, salt, pepper, and tarragon. Stir in the scallions and pasta.

5. Scrape the mixture into a quiche dish. Lightly stir in the Gruyère. Smooth with a spatula. Bake for 40 minutes, until firm. Serve hot or at room temperature.

VAMPIRE REPELLENT

In Central and Eastern Europe, garlic was considered a vampire repellent. The belief was that if enough garlic was stuffed into the bloodsucker's mouth and heaped into the coffin before burial, he would not rise again. The aromatic bulbs also repelled werewolves and were used to protect freshly made butter from elves.

SAVORY NOODLE KUGEL

♣ There are both sweet and savory versions of noodle kugel (pudding). Either way they are great favorites at Jewish holiday feasts. This can be made a day in advance and gently reheated at serving time. Its puffiness will have subsided, of course, and it will not be quite as spectacular as in its glory, but it will still be quite good.

Serves 8

¼ pound unsalted butter
6 cloves garlic, coarsely chopped
4 large onions, coarsely chopped
8 ounces wide egg noodles, uncooked
4 eggs, separated, at room temperature
8 ounces creamed cottage cheese, at room temperature
1 cup sour cream, at room temperature
Salt and freshly ground pepper to taste

1. Preheat oven to 350° F.

2. Melt the butter. Toss in the garlic and onions. Cover and let steam over very low heat for 15 minutes. Uncover, raise heat a bit, and cook, stirring occasionally, until the onions are a deep amber brown. (The preliminary steaming will subdue the garlic and prevent it from turning bitter.)

3. Cook the noodles *al dente*.

4. Drain the noodles, rinse, and drain again. Toss in a large bowl with the butter-onion mixture.

5. Beat the egg yolks. Beat in the cheese, sour cream, and a liberal amount of salt and pepper. Stir mixture into noodles.

6. In a clean bowl, with a clean beater, beat the egg whites until they hold stiff peaks. Fold the beaten egg whites into the noodle mixture.

7. Pour the noodles into a buttered 1½-quart shallow baking dish. Bake in the preheated oven for 40 to 45 minutes or until puffed and golden.

8. Serve at once.

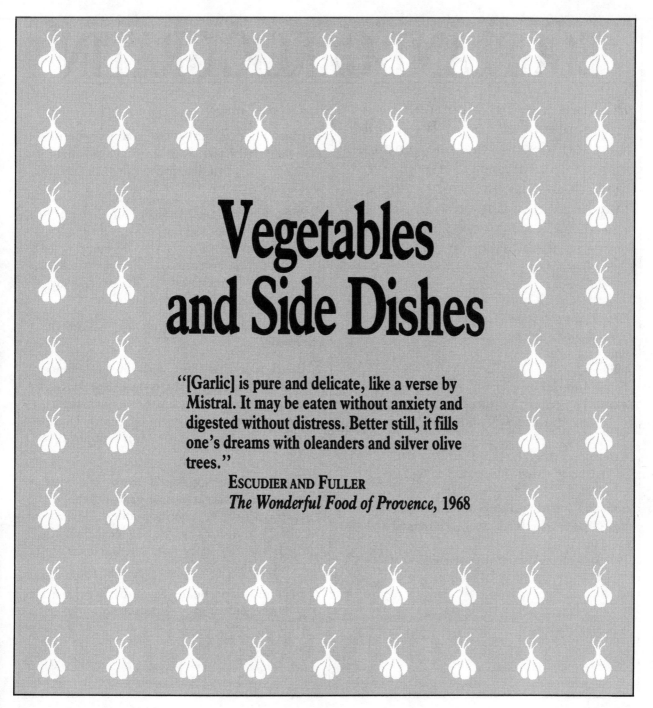

Vegetables and Side Dishes

"[Garlic] is pure and delicate, like a verse by Mistral. It may be eaten without anxiety and digested without distress. Better still, it fills one's dreams with oleanders and silver olive trees."

ESCUDIER AND FULLER
The Wonderful Food of Provence, 1968

EGGPLANT-GARLIC GRATIN

♣ This is a sort of supersophisticated eggplant Parmesan. It's much too good to serve as an accompaniment to a meat dish. Serve it as a main dish in its own right. This may be made a day or so in advance. Reheat, covered, in a 350° F. oven for about ½ hour.

Serves 6

2 medium eggplants, unpeeled, sliced into
    ¼-inch-thick rounds
Salt
Olive oil
1 medium onion, coarsely chopped
2 cans (1 pound 12 ounces each) plum tomatoes, drained well and crushed with the hands
1 teaspoon dried basil, crumbled
½ teaspoon dried thyme, crumbled
1 bay leaf
Salt and freshly ground pepper to taste
2½ cups Garlic Béchamel (see page 19), not too thick
½ cup grated Parmesan cheese

1. Preheat broiler.

2. Place the eggplant slices in a nonreactive (see page 10) bowl. Salt liberally and mix with the hands to distribute salt. Let stand to sweat for ½ hour.

3. Meanwhile, heat 1 tablespoon olive oil in a heavy pan. Sauté the onion until limp and golden. Add tomatoes, basil, thyme, bay leaf, salt and pepper. Bring to a boil, reduce heat, and simmer, uncovered, for about ½ hour, until the sauce is thick and chunky.

4. Rinse and drain the eggplant and dry the slices well.

5. Brush a baking sheet with olive oil. Place one layer of eggplant slices on the prepared pan. Broil for 3 to 5 minutes on each side. Repeat with the remaining eggplant. Do not let the slices burn. Adjust oven temperature to 350° F.

6. Place half the eggplant slices on the bottom of a 2-quart lasagna pan or gratin dish. Spread with the crushed tomatoes. Cover with the remaining eggplant slices. Pour the garlic béchamel sauce over all. Sprinkle with the grated Parmesan.

7. Bake in the preheated oven until golden brown and bubbling, 45 minutes to 1 hour.

SHAWM'S GARLIC-STUFFED ONIONS

This is my son's delicious concoction. He was disappointed to discover that stuffing a blanched, hollowed-out onion with softened garlic is part of Provençal cookery, but this combination of ingredients is strictly his own and very different from the traditional Provençal recipe.

Serves 4

6 dried apricot halves, coarsely chopped
2 tablespoons raisins
4 medium onions
20 cloves garlic, parboiled and peeled
2 tablespoons pine nuts
2 tablespoons chopped fresh parsley
2 tablespoons chopped fresh mint
2 tablespoons olive oil
Salt and freshly ground pepper to taste

1. Soak the apricots and raisins in warm water to cover.

2. Preheat the oven to 400° F.

3. Boil the onions in water to cover for 3 minutes. Drain.

4. Cut a small slice from the bottom of each onion so it has a solid base to stand on. Cut a larger slice from the top, remove the skin, and hollow out the onion, leaving a thin shell. Reserve the onion trimmings.

5. Simmer the garlic in water to cover for 15 minutes. Drain.

6. Chop the onion trimmings coarsely. In the container of a food processor combine the trimmings with the garlic, pine nuts, parsley, mint, and oil. Process to a rough paste.

7. Drain the raisins and apricots and add them to the mixture. Season to taste with salt and pepper.

8. Stuff the onions with the garlic mixture, mounding it neatly over the top. Oil a baking dish that can hold the onions comfortably. Place the onions in the dish and bake, uncovered, for 25 to 30 minutes, until the onions are very tender, browned on the bottom, and sizzling. Serve at once.

GRATIN OF POTATOES AND CHEESE

♣♣ Danger! This dish is addictive. It's good hot, cold, and in between. It's good for dinner, for breakfast, or at midnight. Alas, it's hellishly fattening.

Serves 8

2 large cloves garlic, peeled and split
4 large Idaho potatoes, sliced paper-thin
   (slice at the last minute so that they do
   not darken; do not soak in cold water)
Salt and freshly ground pepper to taste
2 cups grated Gruyère cheese
2 pints whipping cream

1. Preheat oven to 325° F.

2. Rub the bottom and sides of a gratin dish with the cut sides of the garlic. Leave the garlic in the dish.

3. Cover with a layer of the potatoes. Sprinkle on some salt, pepper, and cheese. Pour some cream over the whole thing. Repeat until all the potatoes, cream, and cheese are used.

4. Place the pan, uncovered, in the oven. (Put a baking sheet underneath to catch spills.) Bake for 1 hour or more, until the top is browned and the cream has cooked down to a thick sauce. During the first ½ hour of cooking, use a broad spatula to push the top layer of potatoes into the cream every once in a while. Serve hot, at room temperature, or cold.

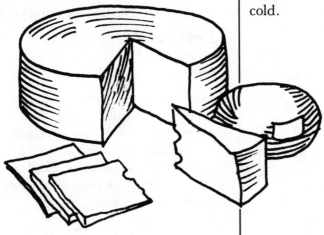

GARLICKY ROAST POTATOES

🧄 Diners mash down on the garlic, so that the purée pops out and is eaten with the potatoes. The Café Plaza, where this dish is served, is in the Copley Plaza Hotel in Boston.

Serves 4

4 Idaho potatoes, peeled and quartered
Salt and freshly ground pepper to taste
12 cloves garlic, unpeeled
¼ pound unsalted butter

1. Preheat oven to 400° F.

2. Boil the potatoes in salted water for exactly 10 minutes. Drain.

3. Place the potatoes in a roasting pan just large enough to accommodate them without crowding. Season with salt and pepper. Scatter in the unpeeled garlic cloves and dot the potatoes with butter.

4. Roast in the preheated oven for 30 minutes, or until well browned and cooked through, turning the potatoes once or twice to assure even roasting.

STIR-FRIED CAULIFLOWER

🧄🧄 My favorite treatment of cauliflower is stir-frying. It tastes wonderful when browned in the garlic-flavored butter, but do not allow it to become overcooked. It must retain a hint of crispness.

Serves 4–6

1 large head cauliflower, trimmed and separated into flowerets
1½ tablespoons unsalted butter
1½ tablespoons vegetable oil
3 cloves garlic, peeled and crushed
Salt and freshly ground pepper to taste

Chopped fresh parsley

1. Steam the cauliflower over boiling water for 3 minutes. Plunge into cold water and drain. Set it aside until needed.

2. Heat the butter and oil in a wide, heavy skillet or wok. Sauté the crushed garlic in the butter until pale golden. Scoop out with a slotted spoon and discard—or reserve for a private nibble.

3. Add the cauliflower and stir-fry over moderate heat until nicely browned and tender but not mushy. Season with salt and pepper, sprinkle with chopped parsley, and serve at once.

GARLIC SOUFFLE

A lovely soufflé, from Chez Panisse, the famous Berkeley restaurant that did so much to put garlic on the American culinary map.

Serves 6–8

Purée from 1½ heads Roasted Garlic (recipe
    follows)
1½ cups half-and-half
1 cup whipping cream
1 slice onion
1 small bay leaf
1 sprig parsley
⅛ teaspoon thyme
5 tablespoons unsalted butter
⅓ cup flour
½ teaspoon salt
⅛ teaspoon white pepper
$1/16$ teaspoon cayenne
5 egg yolks, lightly beaten
1 cup grated Gruyère cheese (3 ounces)
½ cup grated Parmesan cheese plus 1 table-
    spoon for topping
6 egg whites (¾ cup)

"Garlic is the best aphrodisiac in the world."
ROBERT CHARLES
1977

1. Preheat oven to 350° F.

2. Prepare roasted garlic purée.

3. Combine half-and-half, cream, onion, bay leaf, parsley, and thyme and heat slowly to scalding, then set aside.

4. Melt the butter in a large saucepan, stir in the flour and cook over low heat for 3 to 4 minutes, stirring. Remove from the heat. Slowly pour the hot cream mixture through a strainer into a pan to remove the onion and herbs, stirring. Return the mixture to the heat and cook, stirring, until it comes to full boil and thickens.

5. Turn the heat low and cook for 3 to 4 minutes. Stir in the garlic purée, salt, pepper, and cayenne. Stir a little bit of the hot mixture into the egg yolks, then turn the egg yolks into the remaining hot mixture, add the cheeses, and stir until melted. Set aside.

6. Beat the egg whites until they are stiff but not dry. Thoroughly fold about ¼ of the egg whites into the soufflé mixture. Gradually fold in the remainder.

7. Turn the mixture into a 2-quart soufflé dish fitted with a 3-inch foil collar. Sprinkle with 1 tablespoon additional Parmesan cheese.

8. Bake at 350° F. for 30 to 35 minutes, until well puffed and golden brown. Remove collar and serve at once from baking dish.

Roasted Garlic Purée:

This garlic purée, which becomes very mild, requires little attention and can be made early in the day. To halve the soufflé recipe, cut all ingredients by half (3 egg yolks instead of 2 will not matter) and use a 1½ quart soufflé dish without a foil collar (or use a deep latter or shallow baking dish as is often done at Chez Panisse.)

Makes 2 tablespoons purée

1 ½ large heads fresh garlic
1 tablespoon olive oil
1 small bay leaf
⅛ teaspoon thyme
¼ cup water

1. Combine ingredients

2. Bake at 250° F. for 1½ hours, stirring occasionally and basting garlic as liquid is reduced.

3. Remove from oven and press through a sieve, discarding skins.

GRATIN OF CABBAGE

Cabbage delights me, although literary tradition insists that it is an odiferous and poverty-stricken vegetable. On the contrary, cabbage, when cooked properly (which means not overcooked), is crisp and delicious.

Serves 4–6

6 tablespoons unsalted butter
1 medium cabbage, cored, trimmed of tough outer leaves, halved, and sliced into strips
2 ½ cups Garlic Béchamel (see page 19)
1 cup grated Gruyère cheese, Parmesan cheese, or a combination of both

1. Preheat oven to 400° F.

2. Heat the butter in a deep, heavy pot. Toss the cabbage in the hot butter until it is crisp-tender. (It must, under no circumstances, get mushy.) It will overflow the pot at first and then greatly reduce in volume as it cooks.

3. Fold together the cabbage and garlic béchamel. Pour the mixture into a 2-quart shallow baking dish. Sprinkle with cheese.

4. Bake in the preheated oven, uncovered, for 20 to 30 minutes, until browned and bubbly.

GARLIC-WINE RICE PILAF

Serves 4

Rind of 1 lemon
8 cloves garlic, peeled
½ cup parsley
6 tablespoons unsalted butter
1 cup rice (neither instant nor converted)
1¼ cups chicken stock
¾ cup dry vermouth
Salt and freshly ground pepper to taste

1. Chop together the lemon rind, garlic, and parsley.

2. Heat the butter in a heavy 2-quart pot. Cook the garlic mixture very gently for 10 minutes.

3. Stir in the rice. Stir over medium heat for 2 minutes.

4. Combine the stock and wine in a saucepan. Heat until it begins to bubble at the sides. Stir into the rice; add salt and pepper. Cover tightly and simmer over very low heat for 20 to 30 minutes, or until liquid is absorbed and rice is tender. Fluff with a fork.

5. Drape a towel over the pot and cover the towel until it is time to serve. Serve hot or at room temperature.

RICE WITH GARLIC AND PINE NUTS

The pairing of rice and garlic, two ancient foodstuffs, seems like a natural one, whether the garlic is gentle, as in this recipe, or pungent, as in the next.

Serves 6–8

4 tablespoons unsalted butter
Purée from 1 head Roasted Garlic (see pages 14-15)
4 cups cooked rice (use neither instant nor converted)
¾ cup pine nuts
Salt and freshly ground pepper to taste

1. Heat the butter in a wide skillet. Swirl in the garlic purée.

2. Add the rice and pine nuts. Sauté, stirring and tossing, until the rice is heated through and has absorbed the butter. Season to taste. Serve at once.

GARLICKY BREAD AND CHEESE PUDDING

🧄🧄 Bread puddings are very soufflé-like, with none of a soufflé's temperament. This one may be put together the night before, covered with plastic wrap, and refrigerated. Bring to room temperature before baking.

Serves 6

6 ounces day-old French or Italian bread, cut into 1-inch cubes
¼ pound unsalted butter
4 cloves garlic, crushed
½ cup thinly sliced scallions, green and white parts
½ cup chopped fresh parsley
1 teaspoon fresh thyme (or ¼ teaspoon dried)
1 cup grated Gruyère cheese
4 eggs
2½ cups milk
2 tablespoons Dijon mustard
Salt and freshly ground pepper to taste

1. Preheat oven to 350° F.

2. Place the bread in a ceramic 1½-quart soufflé dish or a deep 10-inch quiche dish.

3. Melt the butter in a skillet. Sauté the garlic and scallions until tender but not browned and pour the mixture over the bread cubes.

4. Scatter the parsley, thyme, and cheese over the butter-soaked bread.

5. Beat the eggs. Beat in the milk, mustard, salt and pepper. Pour the egg mixture over the bread. Push the bread down into the mixture. Let soak for at least 20 minutes.

6. Place in the oven for 45 minutes to 1 hour (the longer time for the soufflé dish) or until a knife inserted in the center comes out clean and the pudding is puffed and golden. Serve at once.

"The effect of garlic, eaten in lumps as an accompaniment to bread and cheese, is naturally awful, but garlic used as it should be used is the soul, the divine essence of cookery."

MRS. W. G. WATERS
The Cook's Decameron, 1920

WILD RICE WITH ORIENTAL MUSHROOMS

🧄This is an ethnic mishmash. The wild rice is an American grass, gathered by American Indians, the seasonings and mushrooms are Oriental, and the garlic cloves are added for the pure "alliumaniacal" joy of it. There is no other food in the world quite like wild rice; it has a texture and taste that is unique. The aquatic grains (not rice at all) should be cooked until they puff and open. Some of the grains will remain closed; it is the contrast between the two that gives a dish of wild rice such wonderful texture. Never overcook it—it must remain *al dente* to be interesting. And be flexible with the cooking time— some batches cook faster than others. Cooked wild rice will keep in the refrigerator, tightly covered, for 2 weeks.

Serves 4–6

1 head leaf lettuce
1 ounce large dried shitake mushrooms, about 5 (available in Oriental groceries)

1½ tablespoons peanut oil
½ cup sliced green onions, green and white parts, plus ¼ cup additional for garnish
1 thin slice fresh ginger, peeled and minced
1 tablespoon dry sherry
1½ teaspoons sugar
¼ cup chicken stock
2 tablespoons soy sauce
2 cups cooked Wild Rice (recipe follows)
¼ cup diced water chestnuts
20 cloves garlic, parboiled, peeled and simmered in stock to cover for 15 minutes
Salt and freshly ground pepper to taste

1. Wash the lettuce thoroughly and separate into leaves. Trim off the tough stem from each leaf and cut each leaf in half. Wrap in a towel and refrigerate until serving time.

2. Rinse dried mushrooms. Soak in warm water to cover for ½ hour. Drain and squeeze dry. Trim off tough stems. Cut the mushrooms into 1-inch squares.

3. Heat the oil in a wide, heavy skillet or wok. Sauté the ½ cup green onions for a few seconds. Add ginger and mushrooms. Stir-fry for 30 seconds.

4. Combine the sherry, sugar, stock, and soy sauce and pour it over the mushroom mixture. Simmer until the liquid is almost all absorbed.

5. Stir in the wild rice, water chestnuts, and garlic. Stir and cook for a few moments to heat through. Add salt and pepper to taste, but go easy on the salt since soy sauce is salty.

6. Unwrap the lettuce leaves. Arrange in a circle on a large platter. Spoon the hot wild rice mixture in a mound in the center. Sprinkle with the green onion garnish. Each diner takes a piece of lettuce, spoons some rice onto it, and eats it like a taco.

Basic Method for Cooking Wild Rice

Makes 3 cups cooked wild rice

1 cup raw wild rice
3 cups stock
Salt

1. Place the rice in a sieve. Rinse briefly under cold running water.

2. Put the rice into a deep saucepan with the stock. Bring to a boil, uncovered, stirring frequently.

3. Reduce heat, cover, and simmer, stirring occasionally, until many of the grains have opened and the unopened grains are *al dente*. The cooking time will vary with the wild rice, so taste as it cooks. The approximate cooking time is 30 to 50 minutes.

4. Drain the wild rice and return it to the pot. Drape a kitchen towel over the pot, put the cover over the towel, and let it sit until ready to serve or use in a recipe. Wild rice prepared in this manner is delicious tossed in butter with sautéed mushrooms, scallions, pine nuts, cubes of ham or shrimp. Don't season it too aggressively; the lovely natural taste of the grain must shine through.

"First, he fastened up the windows and latched them securely; next, taking a handful of the flowers, he rubbed them all over the sashes, as though to ensure that every whiff of air that might get in would be laden with the garlic smell."

BRAM STOKER
Dracula

GARLIC BREAD

Bread baking is easy, and there is no kitchen activity that is more fulfilling, particularly if you use your hands to knead. This garlic bread has the garlic baked right into the dough. You may add Parmesan or Gruyère cheese to the garlic butter; you may use all white flour; or you may brush the top with egg white in lieu of water and sprinkle with poppy seeds.

Makes 3 loaves

Purée from 2 heads Roasted Garlic (see pages 14-15)
¼ pound unsalted butter, softened
2 packages yeast
½ cup warm water (100° F.–115° F.)
2½ cups warm water
2 tablespoons Kosher salt
3¼ cups whole-wheat flour
3¼ cups unbleached white flour
Cornmeal

1. Cream together the garlic purée and butter. (This may be done days in advance and refrigerated. Bring to room temperature before using.)

2. Combine the yeast with ½ cup warm water in a large bowl. Stir with a fork or small whisk. Add an additional 2½ cups water. Add salt.

3. Stir in the flour 1 cup at a time, beginning with the whole wheat. Use a whisk until the dough becomes stiff, then switch to a wooden spoon.

4. Turn the dough onto a well-floured work surface. Knead rhythmically for 10 to 15 minutes, until the dough is smooth, springy, nonsticky, and elastic. Add more flour as you knead if necessary. The dough is ready if you can poke two fingers into it and the resulting indentations spring back.

5. Cover the dough with a cloth and let rest while you wash, dry, and generously butter the bowl. Knead the dough a few more turns, then form it into a ball and place it in the bowl. Turn it to coat with butter. Cover the bowl and put it in a warm, draft-free place until the dough has doubled in bulk, about 1½ hours. It has risen sufficiently when you can gently poke a finger into the dough and the hole remains. (Don't poke too enthusiastically or the dough will collapse.)

6. When doubled, flour your fist and punch the dough down. Knead it a few times and then let it rest.

7. Sprinkle 1 large or 2 small baking sheets with a liberal amount of cornmeal. Divide the dough into 3 equal parts. While you work with 1 piece, keep the other 2 covered. Flour your work surface. With a rolling pin, roll each piece of dough into a rectangle approximately 14 inches long and 7 inches wide.

Spread it with softened garlic butter. Roll the long edge toward the opposite long edge, as if you were rolling up a rug. Pinch ends closed. Place loaves on the baking sheets. With a sharp knife, slash the loaves lightly at 2-inch intervals. Cover with a cloth and place in a warm, draft-free place to rise until doubled, about ½ hour. Meanwhile, preheat oven to 400° F.

8. Bake for 35 to 50 minutes in the oven with a pan of boiling water on the oven floor. Spray the loaves with water several times during the baking process. (The water helps the bread get crusty.) To test for doneness, rap the loaf with your knuckles. The loaf should sound hollow. Cool on wire racks, but these loaves are delicious eaten warm right out of the oven.

GARLIC BAKED POTATOES

The best way to bake potatoes is to bake them too long (if you can bear to leave the oven at 450° F. for 2 hours). The potato skin turns crunchy and the inside becomes amazingly creamy. I love these unadorned—no salt, no pepper, no sour cream—but you may add those traditional garnishes if you wish, or anything else that sounds good: a dollop of pesto or yogurt, a shower of grated Gruyère or Fontina cheese, a scattering of crumbled crisp bacon, or, for a very special treat, a spoonful of garlic purée and a spoonful or two of buttermilk.

1 potato for each person

Large Idaho baking potatoes
Large garlic cloves, split in half

1. Preheat oven to 450° F.

2. Prepare 1 potato for each person. Scrub the potato and dry it well. Prick it in several places with a thin skewer.

3. Rub each potato thoroughly with the cut sides of the split garlic cloves.

4. Place potatoes directly on the oven rack. Bake for 2 hours.

5. Use a good, sharp, serrated knife to cut into the potatoes. The skin will be very hard and crunchy. Serve at once.

GARLIC GRITS

🧄Yankees usually approach their first plate of grits with trepidation. Inevitably they turn away after the first taste, muttering darkly about library paste. They don't know what true Southern grit lovers have always known: that grits are the most delicious, filling, and soul-satisfying of foods. Garlic, cheese, and grits combine to make a traditional Southern dish, although the use of stock, roasted garlic, and Gruyère cheese create a rather unconventional rendition. Leftovers of this dish are unbelievably delicious at about 2:00 in the morning, eaten right out of the refrigerator.

Serves 6

1 cup quick-cooking grits (do not use instant)
3 cups boiling chicken stock
¼ pound (1 stick) unsalted butter cut into pieces, plus some extra butter for greasing casserole
Salt and freshly ground pepper to taste
Pinch cayenne pepper
Purée from 1 head Roasted Garlic (see pages 14-15)
1 cup milk
4 large eggs
1 cup grated Gruyère cheese
1½ tablespoons grated Parmesan cheese

1. Preheat oven to 350° F.

2. Stir the grits into the boiling stock. Cook over medium heat, stirring frequently, until thick.

3. Remove from the heat. Stir in the butter, salt, peppers, and garlic and stir until the butter is melted.

4. Beat the milk into the eggs. Slowly add the milk mixture to the grits and mix well. Fold in the Gruyère cheese.

5. Grease a shallow 2½-quart casserole with softened butter. Sprinkle in the Parmesan and turn the dish to coat the bottom and sides with the cheese. Pour in the grits. Bake for 45 minutes or until puffed and firm. Serve at once.

Salads and Sandwiches

"We absolutely forbid its [garlic] entrance into our salleting [salad] by reasons of its intolerable rankness, which made it so detested of old, that the eating of it was part of the punishment of such as had committed the horrid'st crimes."

JOHN EVELYN, b. 1620

GARLIC BROCCOLI SALAD

♣♣Another version of broccoli and garlic, this time American-style, from The American Café a restaurant in Washington, D.C.

Serves 4

1 large bunch broccoli
⅓ cup mayonnaise, homemade if possible
2 teaspoons chopped garlic
Salt and freshly ground pepper to taste
Grated rind of ½ lemon

1. Remove the heavy stems from the broccoli and peel them. Cut stems into ½-inch slices. Cut the remaining broccoli into bite-size pieces.

2. Steam the broccoli over boiling salted water for 4 to 6 minutes or until tender but still crisp. Plunge the broccoli into cold water to stop cooking, then drain and chill.

3. Mix the broccoli with the remaining ingredients, adding enough mayonnaise to coat the broccoli. Chill until ready to serve.

MUSTARD-GARLIC VINAIGRETTE

Makes about 1 ½ cups

2 tablespoons Dijon mustard
Purée from 1 head Roasted Garlic (see pages 14-15)
⅓ cup wine vinegar
½ cup olive oil
½ cup corn oil
Salt and freshly ground pepper to taste

1. With a small wire whisk, beat together the mustard and garlic purée.

2. Beat in the vinegar.

3. Whisking slowly, add the oils in a thin stream. The mixture will be thick, creamy, and emulsified.

4. Beat in a very frugal amount of salt and pepper. (You may feel that it needs none at all.)

5. Serve with greens, or, for a special first course, serve with new potatoes, steamed in their skins.

GREEN SALAD WITH ORANGES

🧄🧄Oranges, onions, and garlic are soul mates. Try this delicious salad. For a simpler salad, arrange sliced, peeled oranges in a bowl; top with thinly sliced onion rings and sprinkle with chopped garlic. Moisten with a vinaigrette and marinate for several hours.

Serves 6

½ cup olive oil
¼ cup white wine vinegar
¼ cup dry vermouth
3 cloves garlic, crushed
Salt and freshly ground pepper to taste
4 cups mixed greens, washed, dried, and
 torn into bite-size pieces
2 navel oranges
1 large sweet onion, coarsely chopped
½ pound mushrooms, sliced
1 green pepper, coarsely chopped
1 red pepper, coarsely chopped (if unavailable, use ½ cup chopped pimientos or
 roasted red peppers from a jar)
6 strips very crisp bacon, crumbled
½ cup chopped fresh parsley
¼ cup chopped fresh cilantro (Chinese parsley)

1. Combine oil, vinegar, vermouth, garlic, salt, and pepper in a screw-top jar. Shake well. Allow to marinate for several hours.

2. Choose romaine, red-leaf lettuce, escarole, young tender spinach leaves—anything but iceberg. The greens must be cold and very dry. Arrange them in a bowl.

3. Peel the oranges over a small bowl to catch their juice. Remove and discard all the white pith. Section the oranges and halve each section. Add to the greens (add reserved orange juice to dressing mixture).

4. Add onions, mushrooms, peppers, bacon, and herbs to the greens.

5. Toss the dressing into the salad. Serve at once.

GREEN BEAN SALAD

🧄🧄🧄 The beans are crisp, the garlic-anchovy paste is pungent, and the whole effect is earthy. This salad may be prepared ahead and stored in the refrigerator. Allow the beans to come to room temperature before serving.

Serves 6

2 pounds green beans, trimmed
6 cloves garlic, crushed
1 2-ounce can anchovy fillets, drained
1 tablespoon wine vinegar
½ cup olive oil
Freshly ground pepper to taste
¼ cup grated Parmesan cheese
Watercress
Black olives
Tomato wedges

1. Steam the beans over boiling water until crisp-tender. Plunge into very cold water. Drain and set aside.

2. Chop the crushed garlic and anchovies together until they form a paste. Scrape the paste into a bowl.

3. With a wire whisk, beat in the vinegar, olive oil, and pepper.

4. Toss the beans with the dressing. Sprinkle in the Parmesan cheese.

5. Allow the beans to marinate for an hour at room temperature.

6. Arrange the beans on a platter. Garnish with watercress, olives, and tomato wedges.

LEMON-GARLIC VINAIGRETTE

Makes about ½ cup

6 tablespoons olive oil
2 tablespoons white wine vinegar
Juice of ½ lemon
2 garlic cloves, peeled and crushed
Salt and freshly ground pepper to taste

Combine all the ingredients in a screw-top jar. Allow to sit for an hour or so before serving. Shake well before using.

BEEF, MUSHROOM, AND CHEESE SALAD

❦ Main-dish salads make wonderful warm-weather suppers. This salad of rare beef, Swiss cheese, and lightly sautéed mushrooms bathed in a mustardy-garlicky dressing is substantial and good.

Serves 6

1 flank steak (about 1½ pounds)
Salt and freshly ground pepper to taste
· 3 tablespoons olive oil
1 pound mushrooms, trimmed and sliced
Juice of 1 lemon
½ cup chopped fresh parsley plus additional
    for garnish
½ pound Swiss cheese, cut into ½-inch
    cubes
Mustard-Garlic Vinaigrette (see page 110)
Watercress

1. Sprinkle steak with salt and pepper. Broil or grill for 3 to 4 minutes on each side. The beef should be quite rare. Remove to a platter and set aside.

2. Heat the oil in a skillet. Sauté the mushrooms in the oil with the lemon juice until they are just done. Season with salt and pepper. Set aside in the skillet to cool.

3. Slice the beef thinly. Toss in a bowl with the mushrooms. Reserve both the meat juices and the mushroom juices. Toss the parsley and the cheese into the bowl with the beef and mushrooms. Whisk the reserved meat juices and mushroom juices into the mustard dressing.

4. Toss the dressing into the meat-mushroom mixture and allow to marinate at room temperature for several hours. Sprinkle with additional parsley just before serving, and garnish the platter with watercress. After the initial marination, store this salad in the refrigerator, but allow to warm up a bit, at room temperature, before serving.

OPEN-FACED HAM AND CHEESE SANDWICHES

🧄🧄 It's amazing what just ½ a garlic clove split, rubbed on toast, can do. Try this trick on toasted English muffins and top with a poached egg. It is equally good with prosciutto and provolone.

Serves 6

6 slices cracked wheat bread, toasted
3 cloves garlic, halved
6 slices good quality ham, trimmed to fit
    bread
6 generous slices cheese (Fontina, Jarlsberg,
    Gruyère, or Cheddar)
6 tablespoons melted unsalted butter
6 tablespoons grated Parmesan cheese

1. Preheat broiler.

2. Rub each slice of toasted bread generously with a cut clove of garlic.

3. Place a slice of ham on each slice of bread. Cover with a slice of cheese. Drizzle a tablespoon of melted butter over each and sprinkle with a tablespoon of freshly grated Parmesan cheese.

4. Broil the open-faced sandwiches for 3 to 5 minutes until the cheese is melted and bubbly. Serve at once with knives and forks.

Even Shakespeare cautioned actors to "eat no onions and garlic for we are to utter sweet breath."

WILLIAM SHAKESPEARE
A Midsummer Night's Dream

SAUSAGE AND PEPPERS IN PITA BREAD

♣♣ This classic combination is usually served on Italian loaf bread, but it is fun to serve it with pita bread and an array of interesting garnishes. The most spectacular garnish of all is pesto; if you have a source of fresh basil and make pesto often, include it in this dish.

Serves 6–8

2 tablespoons olive oil
10–12 Italian sausage links, hot, sweet, or a combination
2 large onions, cut in half and sliced into thin half moons
4 peppers, sliced into strips (use half red and half green if possible)
4 garlic cloves, minced
½ cup red wine
1 can (1 pound 12 ounces) plum tomatoes, well drained and chopped
Salt and freshly ground pepper to taste

Garnishes

1½ pounds mushrooms, quartered and sautéed in butter
Pine nuts or coarsely chopped walnuts
Diced bell peppers, green and red
Chopped fresh parsley
Chopped fresh basil
Grated Parmesan cheese
Pesto (see page 21)

1. Heat the oil in a wide, deep, heavy skillet. Prick the sausages in several places with a fork. Sauté over high heat for 5 minutes.

2. Reduce the heat a bit, add the onions, and cook, stirring, for 5 more minutes.

3. Add the peppers and garlic and cook, stirring occasionally, for another 5 minutes.

4. Dump the contents of the skillet into a colander to drain away all the fat. Return the mixture to skillet and pour in the wine. Cook over high heat until wine has almost cooked away.

5. Toss in the tomatoes, season, reduce the heat, and simmer until the sausages are cooked through and the tomatoes are no longer saucy.

6. Cut the sausages into 1-inch pieces. Mound the sausage mixture in a deep platter. Place on the dining table with a basket of pita bread and bowls of garnishes and let the guests make their own sandwiches and their own topping.

YOGURT DRESSING

♣♣This dressing, from The Happy Baker, a Chattanooga, Tennessee, cooking school, is good on mixed greens and with *crûdités,* but it will knock your socks off if used with melon slices, peach slices, or other fresh fruits. With fruit, it's good enough—garlic, horseradish, and all—to serve for dessert.

Makes about 1½ cups

1 cup plain yogurt
¼ cup prepared horseradish, well drained
¼ cup *Crème Fraîche* (see page 57)

1 tablespoon honey
2 teaspoons white wine vinegar
2 cloves garlic, peeled and crushed
2 tablespoons chopped chives or 1 scallion, sliced thin
2 tablespoons chopped fresh basil or 2 teaspoons dried, crushed between the fingers
Salt and freshly ground pepper to taste

1. Place the yogurt in a bowl. Beat in the horseradish and *crème fraîche.*

2. Add the honey, vinegar, garlic, chives, basil, salt and pepper.

3. Refrigerate overnight for the flavors to meld.

TOMATO SANDWICH

♣♣Tomatoes and garlic are one of the simplest and most satisfying of all culinary combinations. But the tomatoes must be fresh and juicy. Save these sandwiches for summer eating.

Serves 3–4

1 long loaf French bread (about 12 inches long)

1 large clove garlic, split in half
1½ tablespoons olive oil
3–4 ripe tomatoes, cored and sliced
Salt and freshly ground pepper to taste
1 tablespoon chopped fresh basil
1 tablespoon chopped fresh parsley (double the amount if fresh basil is unavailable)
1 sweet onion, sliced paper thin

1. Split loaf lengthwise. Rub the inside of each half with the cut side of half a garlic clove. Sprinkle ½ tablespoon of the olive oil over the garlic-rubbed surface of each half.

2. Place the tomato slices down the length of the bottom half. Sprinkle with salt, pepper, basil, and parsley. Arrange sliced onion over tomatoes. Sprinkle the remaining olive oil over all.

3. Cover with the top half of the loaf and press down. Wrap tightly with foil and allow to sit at room temperature for at least 1 hour. The waiting time is essential; this is one sandwich that is *supposed* to be soggy!

TOMATO SALAD SANDWICH

Use the ingredients for tomato sandwich, above, plus:

6 ounces feta cheese, well drained and crumbled
½ cup Greek black olives, halved and pitted

Split the bread, rub with garlic, and sprinkle with oil. Sprinkle feta cheese over the lower half of the loaf. Arrange the tomato slices over the cheese. Season with pepper and herbs (omit salt, as feta is salty) and cover with onion rings and olives. Sprinkle with tablespoon olive oil. Cover with the top half of the loaf and press down. Wrap tightly and allow to ripen for at least 1 hour.

TOMATO AND CHEESE PIZZAS

🧄🧄Italian Fontina cheese is one of the best cheeses in the world. The buttery, pungent cheese is at its best when melted; here it is combined with ripe tomatoes, basil, and garlic-scented olive oil on pita breads—instant (and irresistible) pizza.

Serves 4

2 large cloves garlic, crushed
¼ cup olive oil
4 pita breads

4 medium ripe tomatoes, sliced
1 pound Italian Fontina cheese, sliced
Salt to taste
Chopped fresh basil leaves

1. Combine the oil and garlic. Allow it to marinate for at least 1 hour.

2. Preheat oven to 400° F.

3. Arrange overlapping slices of tomatoes and cheese on each pita bread. Sprinkle with garlic-flavored oil and salt to taste. Sprinkle with basil leaves.

4. Bake for 10 minutes. Cut each pita in quarters. Serve piping hot.

FRANK MA'S GARLIC BROCCOLI

🧄🧄🧄 There is nothing subtle about this Chinese-style broccoli; it packs a garlicky wallop.

Serves 6

2 bunches broccoli
Salt to taste
½ teaspoon sugar
3 cloves garlic, peeled and crushed
2 teaspoons sesame oil

1. Cut the broccoli flowers off the stems. Divide into flowerets. Save remainder of broccoli for another use.

2. Cook the broccoli in boiling water for 60 seconds. Drain and rinse well in very cold water.

3. Mix the cold broccoli with salt, sugar, and garlic. Toss in the sesame oil.

4. Serve at once or refrigerate for a few hours. It is best eaten as soon as possible.

Desserts

"Garlic can be used in practically all nonsweet dishes."

When the Good Cook Gardens, 1974

GARLIC SORBET

♠ This is not a dessert. It's meant to be a refresher served between courses, but it could be served for dessert by decreasing the lemon juice by half. A scoop of this is lovely in a glass of champagne.

Serves 6–8

½ cup garlic cloves, peeled (approximately 25 large cloves)
3½ cups water
1 cup sugar
1 cup dry white wine
1½ tablespoons lemon juice
Fresh mint leaves

1. Combine the garlic and 1½ cups water in a saucepan. Boil, covered, for ½ hour.

2. Prepare a simple syrup: Stir the sugar and the remaining 2 cups water together in a saucepan. Bring to a boil and boil for 5 minutes. Cool.

3. Strain the garlic water. (Reserve the garlic cloves for another use.) Stir together the garlic water, simple syrup, wine, and lemon juice. Pour the mixture into 2 sectioned ice cube trays and freeze for several hours until almost solid. (The cubes will feel slightly spongy rather than solid.) Put a metal bowl in the freezer to chill.

4. Quickly empty the trays into the container of a food processor. Process to a fluffy slush. Quickly scrape into the chilled metal bowl, cover, and return to the freezer to firm up a bit. (It can stay in the freezer, until you are ready to serve it—for days if necessary.)

5. To serve, scoop into glass goblets that have been chilled in the freezer. Garnish with mint leaves and serve at once.

LEMON-GARLIC CREAM

♠ Garlic desserts *are* good. Garlic desserts will not hurt you. It may sound awful and bizarre, but you must trust me. The garlic adds something very special to this creamy dessert, but it is not identifiable as garlic.

Serves 6

4 cups unflavored yogurt
2 cups whipping cream
6 cloves garlic, parboiled and peeled
½ envelope unflavored gelatin
⅛ cup cold water
3 tablespoons lemon juice

½ teaspoon vanilla extract
½ cup sugar
1 teaspoon grated lemon peel plus additional
 for garnish
Freshly grated nutmeg

1. Dump the yogurt into a sieve that has been lined with damp cheesecloth. Place it over a bowl, cover with plastic wrap, and place in the refrigerator to drain for 4 hours.

2. Heat the cream and garlic in a deep, heavy pot. Boil until reduced by ½ cup, about 15 minutes. (You will have 1½ cups of cream left.)

3. Meanwhile, soften the gelatin in cold water.

4. Stir the lemon juice, vanilla, softened gelatin, and sugar into the thickened cream. Allow to cool to room temperature.

5. When cooled, strain it into a bowl. Reserve the garlic. Stir in 1 teaspoon grated lemon peel. Stir in the drained yogurt.

6. Spoon the mixture into 6 dessert goblets. Top each with a clove of the reserved garlic (unless you are afraid that they will frighten your guests; if so, eat them yourself). Sprinkle with grated lemon peel and a bit of grated nutmeg. Chill for several hours.

COCONUT-GARLIC CREAM

Serves 6

1¼ cups milk
6 cloves garlic, parboiled and peeled
1 envelope unflavored gelatin
¼ cup cold water
1 15-ounce can cream of coconut
1 teaspoon vanilla extract
1 cup whipping cream, whipped

1. Heat the milk with the garlic in a deep, heavy saucepan. Simmer together for 15 minutes, until the garlic is tender and the milk is reduced by ¼ cup.

2. Soften the gelatin in the cold water for 5 minutes.

3. Add the gelatin mixture to the milk. Stir until very well combined.

4. Whisk in the cream of coconut and vanilla. Whisk to blend very well. Let the mixture cool to room temperature.

5. Strain the mixture. Reserve the garlic. Chill until the mixture is the consistency of unbeaten egg white.

6. Fold in the whipped cream. Spoon the mixture into 6 stemmed goblets. Chill for several hours. Garnish each serving with a clove of the reserved garlic.

GANACHE GARLIC SAUCE

From Jimella Lucas at The Ark in Nahcotta, Washington, and its garlic festival. Serve this sauce over ice cream. Store it in the refrigerator until needed.

Makes 5 cups

1 pint heavy cream
2 ounces unsalted butter
2 tablespoons sugar
1 pound bittersweet or semisweet chocolate, shredded
¼ cup Garlic Honey (recipe follows)

1. Mix the cream, butter, and sugar in a heavy saucepan. Bring the mixture to a boil.

2. Remove it from the heat and add the chocolate. Stir until melted.

3. Add the garlic honey. Stir well.

4. To serve, warm gently and stir until it becomes pourable.

Garlic Honey

Makes ½ cup

12 garlic cloves, peeled
½ cup honey

1. Combine the garlic and honey in a clear glass jar. Store in a cool, dark place for 1 week to 1 month.

2. Strain the honey through a wire-mesh strainer. Store in a glass jar until needed.

GARLIC AND LOVE

Long ago, wise men of the Talmud believed garlic to be a powerful aphrodisiac. They suggested consumption of large quantities at the Sabbath meal and then the performance of conjugal duties, with vigor and with pleasure, later in the evening.

Source Guide

Placitas Garlic Consortium
Pieroni La Casa Garlic
Star Route Box 66
Placitas, New Mexico 87043

A group of garlic lovers and growers in the Rio Grande Valley.

Gilroy Garlic Festival Association, Inc.
P.O. Box 2311
7365 Monterey Street, Suite E
Gilroy, California 95020

Coordinators of Gilroy's mammoth and joyous annual garlic festival.

La Vieille Maison
Highway 267, P.O. Box 1298
Truckee, California 95734

The one and only garlic-theme restaurant in the United States.

Rapazzini Winery
Highway 101, Box 247
Gilroy, California 95020

The brave and creative inventors of garlic wine.

The Garlic Times
Lovers of the Stinking Rose
1635 Channing Way
Berkeley, California 94703

Garlic-lover Lloyd Harris's impassioned garlic newsletter.

Index